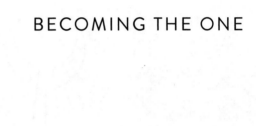

BECOMING THE ONE

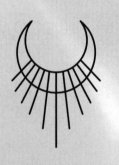

HEAL YOUR PAST, TRANSFORM
YOUR RELATIONSHIP PATTERNS,
and COME HOME TO YOURSELF

BECOMING
THE
ONE

SHELEANA AIYANA

Founder of RISING WOMAN

CHRONICLE PRISM

Library of Congress Cataloging-in-Publication Data

Names: Aiyana, Sheleana, author.

Title: Becoming the one : heal your past, transform your relationship patterns, and come home to yourself / Sheleana Aiyana.

Description: San Francisco, California : Chronicle Prism, [2022] | Includes bibliographical references. | Identifiers: LCCN 2021052189 | ISBN 9781797211671 (hardcover) | ISBN 9781797211695 (ebook)

Subjects: LCSH: Self-consciousness (Awareness) | Love. | Interpersonal relations. | Spiritual life.

Classification: LCC BF575.S4 A39 2022 | DDC 155.2—dc23/eng/20220201

LC record available at https://lccn.loc.gov/2021052189

Manufactured in China.

10 9 8 7 6 5 4 3

Design by Pamela Geismar.

Typesetting by Happenstance Type-O-Rama.

Typeset in Garamond 3 and Brandon Grotesque.

Chronicle books and gifts are available at special quantity discounts to corporations, professional associations, literacy programs, and other organizations. For details and discount information, please contact our premiums department at corporatesales@chroniclebooks.com or at 1-800-759-0190.

CHRONICLE PRISM

Chronicle Prism is an imprint of Chronicle Books LLC, 680 Second Street, San Francisco, California 94107 www.chronicleprism.com

Mom, our souls chose to come together for deeper healing. Thank you for gifting me this life and the experiences I needed to be of service to others. For teaching me generosity and play, and for celebrating my healing path. I love you.

CONTENTS

INTRODUCTION

I AM OFTEN ASKED, "WHAT IS YOUR ADVICE FOR SOME- one who wants to find 'The One'?" Some people are disappointed to hear that I don't subscribe to the typical notion of "The One." This is because, while I fullheartedly believe we can find a partner who connects to us on a soul level, the idea of searching for our "one" holds a major self-limiting message. And that message is that we are somehow incomplete without another.

We are relational beings; we are designed to be in relationship. Deep in our hearts, we all want the experience of true love, yet romantic relationship is not what defines us or makes us whole. This is why my response to anyone who's seeking love is always first to *seek within*. To remember that you are not waiting for confirmation from someone else to know that you are complete.

When we operate from our past wounds or seek external fulfillment, we might approach dating and relationships as if they're a performance. We show up in whatever way we think will impress the other person or keep them interested. But we can't win someone's love by pretending to be someone we're not. Nor should we want to. Instead, when we show up from a space of worth and wholeness, we become "the one" for ourselves.

Over the years, thousands of courageous and incredible women have taken my relationship program Becoming the One. Whether single, in a complicated relationship, or going through heartbreak, wherever they are on their life path, many women ask: "What am I doing wrong? Why do my relationships keep ending?"

Here's the thing: There is nothing wrong with you if you're single or you feel like you can't seem to "get it right" in love. There's nothing wrong with you if you haven't been "chosen."

Many of us grew up on a diet of fairy-tale romance. It was in the books we read, the movies we watched, the advertisements we saw on television—it was and is everywhere we look. We've been taught that we need to be an unrealistic version of "perfection" to be chosen, that somewhere out there is one magical person coming to sweep us off our feet and save us. All the while, we are given texting strategies and game-playing tactics for dating that tell us how we should act and who we should be to make ourselves more attractive.

Somewhere along the way, we learned that to be loved, we had to give ourselves away, turn down our needs, or bend to fit the expectations of others. We are constantly bombarded with messaging that we're not enough or maybe even too much. It all boils down to a culture of *self-abandonment* in the name of trying to find and keep love.

But healthy love doesn't require you to abandon or give yourself away. It doesn't require you to change your core personality or hide your flaws. It does ask you, however, to know yourself at the deepest level, because the truth is that a conscious relationship doesn't begin when you meet a partner. It starts the moment you decide to make your relationship with yourself a priority.

This book is about choosing yourself. It is a reminder to return to the seat of your power and recognize that love is available in many forms. But, in the end, a healthy relationship to self is what fuels all other loves we hope to have in our lives—deep friendships, strong family connections, passion for our work, and romantic love.

In life there is very little we can control outside of ourselves. We don't get to control the timing of when our partners arrive or how long we remain with them. The work is to remain at home in ourselves, no matter what life brings—to claim the right to be joyous and powerful within a relationship or without one.

Becoming the One is your invitation to reclaim the parts of yourself that you may have lost or become disconnected from. It is an inner-work journey to healing and developing a deeper relationship to your own heart. To discover what is important to you—your values, relationship goals, and dreams—so that you can choose love from a place of self-awareness and confidence.

WE ALL HAVE A STORY

My earliest conditioning around love was laced with betrayal, abandonment, and abuse. I spent most of my childhood afraid of men, I never met my father, and I had an emotionally and often physically unavailable mother. Later in life, I found myself attracted to people who were unsafe for me. But even when the alarm bells were going off, I was too conditioned for chaos to choose differently.

By the age of twenty, I had spent many years numbing my pain with hard drugs and alcohol. I had witnessed my mother make multiple attempts to take her own life, lost many close people to suicide and homicide, and endured sexual violence, addiction, homelessness, and domestic abuse. My story is a part of who I am. It has put me on this path, and I'm also aware that my story is just one tiny drop in the ocean of stories of those who have suffered, and continue to, but who will never have the opportunities that I've had to heal and recover.

I want to acknowledge that healing is a gift and a privilege that not everyone has, and it is my hope that each person who heals will find their way of giving back in service to others. By healing ourselves we can contribute to profound change in this world.

My own healing journey didn't truly begin until I was twenty-six years old, catalyzed by a divorce and the stripping away of my own carefully crafted walls and defenses. It was at that time that I met a spiritual teacher whom I journeyed with in Tantra, alchemy, Jungian shadow work, and conscious relationship, and I later became his apprentice. I sat with many Amazonian plant medicines, including rapé (pronounced ha-PAY), kambo, sananga, and psychedelics like DMT and psilocybin, and I eventually found my way to ayahuasca. I prayed, I wrote poetry, and I devoted myself to my healing. I intentionally remained focused on my relationship to self and ignored many date invitations from seemingly attractive suitors to focus on my inner work.

Since then, I have spent thousands of hours in self-study and training in conscious relationship, couples facilitation, family systems work, inherited family trauma, and somatic healing. It was through my own experience of hitting rock bottom and healing my relationship patterns that I came to found Rising Woman, an online community where my team and I provide conscious relationship and self-healing education to millions of people every month.

After years of running Rising Woman and guiding people through my relationship programs, I have come to recognize that many people are caught in a classic dilemma: We may logically know someone isn't right for us, but we still find ourselves pursuing them and the same type of partner again and again.

If you grew up in a family that modeled healthy love and communication, you are the exception, not the rule. Most of us are learning along the way, at the mercy of our conditioning, repeating patterns that ultimately leave us exhausted, bitter, frustrated, or fearful that perhaps love is not in the cards for us.

While our culture is fixated on the idea of breaking or ridding ourselves of patterns, I believe that true change begins when we *integrate and accept* the parts of ourselves that we've hidden, denied, or rejected. By bringing our patterns into awareness, and understanding where they are rooted in our personal history, we can do the work to consciously transform them.

To create the love we want, we have to make space for a new story to emerge. We also have to believe that we are worthy of more. More than that, our body needs to internalize the truth that we are *capable* of creating healthy relationships regardless of what we've experienced or witnessed in our lives.

When we're running on our past conditioning, we might not be able to see our patterns clearly. We might be on a hamster wheel, chasing unavailable love, caretaking, and trying to save people from themselves. Maybe our relationship only lasts a few months before our partner seems to get bored, ghosts, or finds someone else they like more. Maybe we stay longer than we should and put up with far too much. Maybe we're the over-giver, or we struggle to authentically show up as soon as we start to have feelings for someone, all the while abandoning the one who needs us most—ourselves.

If you keep hitting the same wall in dating and relationships, this is not a sign that you are broken. **It is a sign that somewhere along the way, you learned to sacrifice yourself in order to be loved.**

While this is a painful and often frustrating pattern to live in, it's also a sign that you haven't given up on love, and that deep down, some part of you knows in your bones that you can have what you want.

Many of us don't realize that when we sacrifice ourselves or change who we are in order to be loved, we give away our power in relationship. We forget that rather than fighting to be chosen, *we* have the power to choose. In this book, you will learn how to make peace with your past and heal your relationship patterns so that you can be fully expressed and honor the choices you make in relationship, with yourself and others.

A CALL FOR CHANGE

The healing work starts the moment we decide that we never want to go back to the way things were. For some of us, this moment comes when we have reached our lowest point and there's nothing left to grasp on to. For others, it comes when we recognize we can no longer live for someone else, because in doing so we have lost the vital connection to who we are and what our soul craves. These difficult moments, however painful, can be the catalyst for real change.

There is a lot of spiritual medicine in transitional experiences. Before we can release an old chapter of our lives, we must make way for a metaphorical death. That means diving deep into whatever is left to be felt, and then surrendering to what wants to come through, allowing real transformation to occur. **Being in a space of heartache, disappointment, or defeat can be a gift, for it's in these moments that we may be the most open to change.**

It is an opportunity to *break open*. To acknowledge what is not working, and shift directions.

You can't turn back the hands of time and change what happened or prevent your most painful past experiences. But the good news is, your healing does not depend on anyone but you. You do not have to be bound by your past. You can choose a different way forward.

THE PATH TO BECOMING THE ONE

In this book, you will have the opportunity to explore your conditioning, challenge your beliefs about love, and clarify your desires. So that you can consciously choose what *you* want in love and in life.

You will learn the practice of inner-child healing to cultivate self-esteem and internal awareness. Through defining your boundaries and your core values, you'll see how standing firm, speaking up, and showing up authentically help people love you better. You will also develop the tools to reconnect to your body and your intuition, while fostering a relationship with nature and spirit. I will provide simple yet potent meditations and somatic practices that you can use to self-soothe and expand your capacity to ride emotional waves without grasping externally or losing yourself in the process.

Together, we will learn how to embody the qualities and the love we may be seeking in others—or in the perfect partner—and become the one for ourselves. This is the first major step in establishing or attracting a conscious and healthy relationship.

We can't go deep with a partner if we can't go deep with ourselves. We can't hold space for another person if we don't know how to be with our own big emotions. If we're wired to feel turned on by red flags, or if we don't know how to receive love unless we're working hard or abandoning ourselves for it, then we can't truly attract a conscious partnership. To prepare for a conscious relationship, we need to purify our heart and mind of anything that could potentially sabotage our chances of cocreating healthy love.

Relationships are meant to be a space for us to grow, heal, and play in—but they cannot be our everything. You are not defined by your relationship status or your past relationship failures. Every partner you have ever had has the potential to be a teacher for you. But in order to get the message, you have to release yourself from guilt and shame, and accept things as they are.

You deserve to be free and at home in yourself, to know your worth, and to ask for what you want in a relationship. It's not enough to just logically understand "concepts" of conscious relationship; you need to embody them. **Your relationship with yourself is the secure and loving foundation from which you can give and receive love.**

Don't do this work for anyone else. Do it for you. That way, even if the old life dies, a relationship ends, and everything falls apart, you can trust that you are safe, held, and connected to the divine love that resides within us all.

Throughout this book, I share many personal stories from my childhood and adult relationships. My own journey has been full of heartache and loss, but through those experiences I have found my way to liberated self-love, peace, and a vast, vulnerable love with my life partner. Before I could be ready for the marriage I'm in now with my husband, Ben, I had a lot to unpack from my past. In this book I share with you the healing process and the tools I learned along the way, which have inspired the programs behind Rising Woman.

I have also included client stories that show how our past can affect us and what is possible when we find healing. Names and subtle details have been changed to protect my clients' privacy and confidentiality. Seeing ourselves in other people's stories can be deeply healing. It is a reminder that we are never alone in whatever we may be going through.

While I tend to work with women, my work is not gender specific and can apply to any person who engages in a relationship with another human being, regardless of sexual orientation or gender identity. Wherever you are in your life—whether you are single, in a relationship, going through a breakup, or in a painful cycle with dating—the teachings you will learn here span beyond a particular partner or relationship status.

If you're currently in a relationship, you'll find these practices equally beneficial and enlightening, and you can use the teachings in this book to gain clarity on what you want and how to show up more powerfully in your partnership. If you're in a partnership that you're not sure is right for you, this book will also help you find a way forward that's rooted in self-devotion.

I want you to know that you can have whatever your heart and soul desires. It is never too late. My prayer for you is that you will be reunited with that sacred connection to yourself, to nature, and to the wisdom of your own heart. When you arrive in this place, you will remember with every cell of your being that you are and have always been capable and worthy of creating love anchored in reverence and truth.

PART ONE

RECLAIM YOUR RELATIONSHIP TO SELF

Home is not another person or a place outside of you. Home is the love you have within you. It is the remembrance that you are already complete. Yes, even with your wounds. Even with the scars from your past. You don't need to chase love; you need to remember the love that you are.

CHAPTER 1

THE HEALING JOURNEY

WHEN I WAS THREE YEARS OLD, MY MOTHER WAS JUST twenty-five. We lived in a ground-floor basement suite in a cul-de-sac on the edge of a low-income neighborhood. It had two bedrooms and one bathroom with white walls and cream and brown vinyl floors in the kitchen, like many places in the 1980s and '90s. My mother collected glass angel statues and pictures of unicorns and plants, which covered every area of the home from floor to ceiling (I proudly inherited her green thumb). She was a survivor of horrific childhood abuse, and her history was colored by physical and sexual abuse, betrayal, abandonment, and neglect. Because of this, she struggled greatly with depression and undiagnosed C-PTSD (complex post-traumatic stress disorder).

She would frequently sleep during the day and go out drinking at night, leaving me at home alone to be with my imagination. Returning home drunk and sick, she would curl up on the bathroom floor for the night and I would cover her with a blanket. Sometimes, I would bring her a cookie sheet with toothpaste, a toothbrush, and a facecloth, trying my best to take care of her when she was hungover. Other times, she returned home in a rage. She yelled and punched the walls, bringing our photos crashing down onto the ground. I remember sitting in the hallway crying, surrounded by chaos and broken glass with a picture frame in my lap.

I also shared many beautiful moments with my mother. Because she was very childlike emotionally, she really knew how to play and have fun. We would have bubble gum–eating contests and play dress-up or have picnics in the backyard. Regardless of the chaos and lack of emotional nurturance, my mother was my everything, and I loved her deeply. Since I never met my father, we created a little bubble of two, a world of our own. At night, I would often climb out of my bed and crawl into hers, wrapping my arms and legs tightly around her body.

I'll never forget one particular night, a night that would change my entire life and forever alter the meaning of safety and love for me. My mother had bundled me up and put me in the front seat of her car. We drove for what felt like a long time until we came to a large white house and parked in the driveway. My mother left the engine running as she carried me to the doorstep, where a man and a woman I had never met answered the door. Placing me in their arms, she turned and walked back toward her car. I kicked and thrashed, screaming, "Mommy!" until she disappeared into the foggy blare of her headlights, reversing her beat-up, gray hatchback Chevy and driving away into the night. Heartbroken, alone, and afraid, I had this moment time-stamped on my psyche. This moment was the origin of my abandonment wounding. It was the moment my world changed.

Because of this, I moved into my adult relationships wired to ignore red flags. I found myself in a series of unhealthy relationships that mirrored the chaos that had ripped through my childhood. I chased unavailable love and was drawn to people who were, in some way, unsafe to love.

HISTORY REPEATS

I was twenty-six and one year into an unhappy marriage to a person who was a reflection of my inner wounding. We married because we were from different countries (I'm Canadian; he was American) and the borders were starting to threaten us with being blacklisted from travel unless we stopped hopping back and forth. The decision was made with much hesitation. Nothing about it was romantic. Looking back, we weren't really in love; we were just two young people struggling in our relationship and clinging to something that we were too afraid to let go of. Now it's easy to see that we both carried deep wounds from childhood, and we were both profoundly affected by our mothers, and it was from this place that we related to one another.

Our entire relationship was dysfunctional. We constantly fought, had very little sexual chemistry or attraction, and played roles that kept us both stuck. He was the underfunctioning one who was often depressed and riddled with self-doubt, and I was the overfunctioning savior who "had it all figured out" and could take care of everything on my own.

As time went on, I felt more and more trapped, and I couldn't shake the sense that I was living the wrong life. Fantasies of ending the relationship took up a lot of space in my mind, but my arrogance and self-importance kept me there. I believed he needed me. He was often frozen with anxiety, and I was convinced it was up to me to step in with solutions. I caught him stealing and lying, but I consistently turned down my intuition and allowed the discomfort to billow in my body. We ran a business together, but he spent most of his days sleeping until late afternoon or sitting at his computer in the basement. He would complain that he wanted more adventure but we couldn't afford it, and I would feel internal pressure to make more money to give him what he wanted. I took on the burden of the sole provider and held far too much space for his entitlement. We enabled each other to stay in a familiar pattern, which would ultimately be what would break us.

After years of struggling to create chemistry and realizing that things needed to change, we decided to open up our relationship as a last-ditch effort to see if maybe, just maybe, we could make things work and find the passion and love we both wanted. So I bought him a ticket to visit his friends in the United States, and while he was away, he ended up meeting someone who he dated for a while. Surprisingly—or maybe not, given how disconnected I felt from him and our union—I didn't feel much jealousy at all. Instead, I felt relieved. The pressure lessened and I felt like I could breathe again. I could be with myself, away from the tether of responsibility to make sure he was taken care of.

Lying in bed one night with the moonlight peering through the blinds, I stared up at my ceiling and wished that he would fall in love with someone else so that I didn't have to feel the guilt of hurting him. That way, someone else could take care of him and I could be free. The thought of being on my own felt liberating and exciting! I didn't want to live this kind of life anymore, suffocated at every turn.

My wish came true: It wasn't more than a few months later that he developed a fast and passionate connection with a woman we both knew, and that was it. He was gone. They spent every waking moment together. He would come in to grab some things only to leave again. And although I'd asked for this, the little girl within me began to feel abandoned, jealous, and terrified. Suddenly, I wasn't okay with this anymore. All of those nights wishing him away and feeling trapped vanished from my memory and I was overcome with panic and an urgency to win him back. I self-abandoned and lost myself, pursuing him desperately and escalating conflict to the point of no return.

After months of chaos and an explosive argument, one warm summer day he came home to pack his things for the last time while his girlfriend waited outside in her red SUV. I trailed him around the house yelling while he feverishly threw his belongings into bags and bolted out the front door. I followed him outside barefoot and screamed at them to never come back as he hopped into the passenger seat and they sped away. As I stood alone in the middle of our tree-lined street, I was overcome with emotion and fear. He was abandoning our life together, and all of a sudden I was flooded with the memory of my mother placing me in the arms of strangers while I thrashed and screamed, crying for her to please keep me, before she got back in her car and drove away. I was no longer adult me, I was three-year-old me. I felt abandoned, alone, and terrified.

And then, it was as if the crown of my head opened up, and I heard a whisper from deep within: *This is not about him; this is about you.* I felt relief wash over me. Relief that he didn't need to do or be anything in order for me to be okay again. The pain I felt was rooted in past wounds that had been left unattended for far too long. Wounds that secretly held beliefs like *You're not enough. You're permanently broken. Who would want you?* But in that moment, I knew that I had the power within to get myself out of that painful state.

Our separation and eventual divorce were long, drawn out, and painful. I lost everything. My soul-kitty, Maya, whom I had adopted when we lived in California, was taken by coyotes. My ex betrayed me in numerous ways, taking all of my money and leaving me with a pile of debt. I went through the courts to obtain a divorce without his signature after chasing him for years. Upon realizing I was never going to see any of my money again, I cut my losses and accepted that it was time to focus on rebuilding rather than waiting for him to change his behavior.

This is how relationship patterns work. Notice the similarities between my story of early childhood and my first marriage.

It is common to find ourselves faced with familiar emotional themes over and over but unable to recognize that we're in a pattern. Most of us weren't taught that we'd carry our wounds from childhood into our adult relationships or that our greatest relationship challenges, more often than not, come from an unconscious attempt to heal old wounds.

When I first start working with someone on their relationship patterns, they will say things like, "I don't see a pattern at all; they were all so different!" While the content of each relationship may be very different, it's important to focus on the *core emotional themes* we bring into each relationship. Core emotional themes are negative beliefs or stories that follow us wherever we go. For example, the ending of my first marriage mirrored something very familiar to me from my childhood. My core emotional themes were abandonment and betrayal, accompanied by the story that I had to do it all on my own, be the caretaker, and shoulder the burden alone.

Throughout this book, you will learn how to unravel your own relationship patterns and slowly transform them. As you revisit these memories, practice attuning to your body and bring curiosity and compassion to whatever arises. While this process is not easy or comfortable, it's the pathway leading you to embodying your truth and liberation. I'm excited for you to go on this journey into the heart of your own relationship patterns so that you can unwind them and finally claim the life you're here to live.

RELATIONSHIP TO SELF

Let me be very clear: My mission with this book is not to help you find love; it is to remind you of the love that you *are*. It's not that

I don't believe in the beauty of a conscious partnership—I do! It's the spiritual path I am on myself. But all too often, we get caught in the belief that a happy life looks a certain way: Find a partner, get married, have children, and live happily ever after. We tend to put so much of our focus on relationships and attracting a partner that we bend and twist ourselves to be whoever we think we *should* be in order to be loved.

Rather than trying to manifest the perfect partner, I want to encourage you to first look inward. It's time for you to consider falling deeply in love with yourself and to trust that your life has meaning that is unique to you, far beyond social-status symbols. If we focus all our energy outwardly or devote our healing work to the sole intention of finding a romantic relationship, we're still missing the point.

Your relationship with yourself is the most important relationship you will ever cultivate. While we can do everything in our power to create a loving relationship, a partnership we think will last forever could still end. Don't let this scare you. I promise I'm not being cynical. We simply don't know when our time is up, and at the end of the day, the only person we are guaranteed to be in a relationship with from birth to death is ourselves. Rather than fixating on the external, we need to spend time developing our internal relationship and recognize that the love we seek doesn't only exist outside of us.

By coming home to your own personal destiny, you will find the foundation necessary to create the life and relationships you want. So you can experience the quality of connection your heart craves.

To heal the patterns that keep us in a cycle of unhappiness and heartbreak, we first need to strengthen our relationship with ourselves. This is where we will begin the healing work together.

WHAT DOES IT MEAN
TO DO "HEALING WORK"?

Healing is sort of like waking up from a dream. Through a break-up, divorce, or some sort of crisis, an opening for transformation can occur. I rarely meet a person who is inspired to do their healing work when they're having the time of their life. Often, it begins when we are exhausted with a pattern and trying to find a way out. Healing doesn't mean forgetting or erasing our past but rather *integrating* it.

Traumas and painful memories are not just products of our mind; they are held in our body, stored on a cellular level, and even inherited from generations before us. As we begin the healing process together, it's vital to acknowledge that it is not as simple as changing our minds and deciding to be different. Our patterns repeat because they are deeply rooted in our body, and so the path we must walk and the healing work we embark on within these pages is a weaving of body, mind, and spirit.

THE HEALING JOURNEY IS

- Grieving the past and what was lost
- Letting go of stagnant relationships
- Allowing for uncertainty while in the process of transition
- Accepting that we cannot change the past
- Forgiving others and ourselves
- Sitting with big emotions we may have suppressed
- Moving pain, memory, and trauma out of the body
- Acknowledging our deep sensitivity
- Learning how to trust love again
- No longer tying our worth to how much we give or do

- Observing our thoughts and giving our mind less power to control our behavior
- Remembering that we are already whole

The healing path often appears when everything else has been stripped away. When the love has been lost, and the promises broken, when everything we thought we knew has turned to smoke and ash. *It is the moments of deep despair and shatter that prepare us for a more awakened existence.*

YOUR HEALING PATH IS UNIQUE TO YOU

I once had a friend who was "chronically single." No matter what she did, she couldn't get past the three-month mark with anyone, even though she desperately wanted to build a long-term relationship with someone. On the other hand, I was engaged for the second time and having my own struggle: staying in the game once I was in a relationship.

My default mode when I'm triggered is to run or, at the very least, to fantasize about running. My mind tells a glorious fantasy of disappearing into the mountains, living like a hermit in the woods in a little cabin safely hidden away from the world, never to be disturbed again, peacefully, completely, and utterly alone.

My friend, by contrast, had spent over five years suffering in deep aloneness. She looked down on herself for being single and would often tell me that I had no idea how lucky I was to be in a relationship, and how awful it was to be alone. And it's true: I am beyond blessed to have an incredible partner. *But my personal truth is that being in a relationship was more challenging for me at that time because it pushed against my instinct to self-protect and keep others at a distance.* On some level, both of us were living a reality that required the most effort from us—she had to learn how to be whole on her own, and I had to learn how to relax into intimacy rather than push it away.

It turns out that my deepest work was *within* relationship. And, when I finally stopped running and giving in to the urge to escape, what I found instead of my isolation fantasy was a loving marriage and a close community.

We often resist our reality because we get caught up in comparison or longing for something different—we want the opposite of what we have right now; we want what *they* have, or what we believe we should have. But life is your teacher, and no matter your relationship status or circumstance, there is healing available for you right here and now.

I'm inviting you to put the idea to rest that life starts when you have a partner, or that relationships are too scary, or that you're not enough, or that things aren't as they should be. I'm not suggesting that acceptance is easy, or that you can blink yourself into a state of surrender. Nor that your current circumstances aren't challenging, or that you should stop feeling longing or desire. Rather, I'm asking you to begin to notice when you feel these things, and instead of holding on to the belief that you're way off course, consider that for now, you're right where you need to be.

To be honest, I often cringe when this is said without context, especially when we are in pain or experiencing great loss. Tragedy does happen, and it can be utterly devastating. In these moments, it doesn't feel "right" and it doesn't feel like it's happening for a reason, and I do not believe you need to embrace that philosophy. But once we're in the deep end of loss, pain, or heartbreak—we're in it. There's nowhere else to go but within. This is when we're faced with a choice: sink or swim, heart closed or open, bitterness or growth. As we move through our pain with an open mind and the willingness to learn, we may discover meaning in our experiences that we never thought we'd find.

Big change often evokes more change; it's a domino effect. In the process, it's normal to question parts of yourself as you let go of old stories and beliefs. It's normal for some friendships to end; it's normal to discover you need more time alone. With change often comes grief, because for something new to emerge, something else in your life may need to die. Times of transformation ask us to be highly discerning with our energy. Trust yourself and the choices you make during this time. It doesn't need to make sense to anyone but you.

If you're meeting new parts of yourself, create space for the evolution to occur. We're all here with lessons to learn. Some of us may be on the path of learning how to open our hearts and let down our walls in relationship. Some of us may be learning how to love ourselves fully and completely, on our own. Our path might be to be in a relationship, or it might be to be single—perhaps not forever, but for a time—both of which are beautiful.

Healing your relationship patterns is a multilayered process. Your journey is unique to you, your history, and the lessons your soul has come here to learn. Give yourself permission to take it slow; there really is no rush. Step by step, breath by breath. You are healing.

WHAT IT MEANS TO
BECOME THE ONE

A multibillion-dollar personal growth industry has sold us the idea that we need to change who we are to have what we want. We've been taught that attracting a partner requires disingenuous game-playing, and that we need to extract the "undesirable" qualities from our personality to be attractive. As a result, you may have felt torn between being yourself and being who you've been told to be by the outside world.

Becoming the One, and all of my work, is a response to the idea that you need to change or fix who you are in order to be loved. This book is about self-acceptance, because even the parts of yourself that you think are hard to love deserve a seat at the table. This is an opportunity for you to leave all the rest at the door: the pushing, the striving, the perfectionism, the struggling to be anyone other than who you are.

Woven throughout this book are rituals and teachings to connect you to nature—to reawaken to the knowledge that you are one with all living beings. The plants, animals, forests, rivers, oceans, and all of creation are within you. Reconnecting to nature is a doorway to remembering divine and unconditional self-love.

Becoming the One is inspired by my flagship online program. Over 30,000 people in 146 countries have successfully completed the journey, and thousands more begin it each month. I designed this book with three healing intentions in mind:

1. To find your wholeness and deepen a secure and loving relationship with yourself

2. To make peace with your past and heal your wounds

3. To offer a holistic and spiritual reeducation in relationships, creating a more loving foundation to lead from

BECOMING THE ONE IS NOT ABOUT

- Relationship hacks
- Fixing yourself (you're not broken)
- Learning how to fake self-confidence to attract a partner

- Manifesting your soul mate through positive thinking and intention
- Tricks to manipulate a person into wanting to be with you
- Figuring out how to change your partner (past or present)

BECOMING THE ONE IS ABOUT

- Deepening your relationship to self
- Integrating your past by doing the inner work
- Understanding and healing your relationship patterns
- Learning how to show up authentically in a relationship
- Helping you clarify your desires, your core values, and your boundaries
- Doing the foundational work to prepare you for a conscious relationship
- Remembering your oneness with all living beings in this great universe
- Reaching a place of self-acceptance and compassion for all of your past selves

A FEW THINGS TO KEEP IN MIND DURING THE PROCESS

Be Gentle with Your Heart

While you're navigating this work, you may discover parts of yourself that have been hidden away for a very long time. You may also encounter uncomfortable feelings like shame, guilt, and sadness. Sometimes, just before we're about to have a healing moment, we hit a wall and give up. We put the book back on the shelf and go back to what we were doing before those feelings arose. Please know that it's okay to feel uncomfortable along the way. These feelings simply mean you care, so take some rest and then keep going.

Consider Taking a Break from Alcohol and Substances

While you're exploring your past and confronting your relationship patterns, it's wise to have a high degree of discernment with your well-being. Remove anything that can bring your energy down or put you into a lower state. Consider taking a break from alcohol and other substances (if they're a part of your life) and exchange them for water, herbal teas, whole foods, and more time connecting to the elements—oceans, rivers, forests, mountains, and gardens can all be healing sanctuaries.

Make Yourself a Priority

Throughout this process it is important to embrace alone time, practice self-care, and make yourself a priority. If you tend to over-give, or play the role of caretaker for your friends, family, or partners, this is a reminder to give to *yourself* first. In order to learn how to feel safe in your body and secure in your worth you need to be tuned in to your needs and prioritize your well-being.

Keep a Journal

The exercises and writing prompts included within this book are here to support you in finding your way toward your truth. I suggest starting a journal that accompanies your reading, so you can follow the prompts provided and explore or revisit whatever may arise as you move through the chapters.

Find a Reading Buddy or Start a *Becoming the One* Book Club

You may have one or more friends you'd like to embark on this journey with. Setting up weekly tea dates to discuss what you learn or organizing a book club can be supportive ways to go through this program.

Let Go of the Timeline

There's no rush to have everything figured out or to be perfectly healed. Treat this inner work with reverence and embrace your healing as a lifelong practice. There is always more to learn. Take the pressure off of yourself to get anywhere fast, and let this unfolding be a slow, gentle, and nurturing process.

Make Room for More Joy

Don't let the idea of healing become an obsession. While it's beautiful that so many of us are taking on the deep inner work of clearing our past traumas and removing the blocks we've been carrying for generations, we also need to be mindful not to become so focused on healing that we forget what it's all for: experiencing more joy and connection! Make room for play and laughter and acknowledge yourself for each step you take along the way.

Explore Your Spirituality

This is an opportunity for you to remember your connection to Spirit. My use of the term *Spirit* throughout these pages is in reference to the source of vast and unconditional love that exists within and all around each of us. We can feel this connection in our dream space, in meditation, and when we're immersed in nature. Some feel more comfortable using the terms *God*, *Source Energy*, or *Mother Nature*. Please note that I am not speaking in a religious context here, and you are free to explore what your personal relationship to Spirit looks like.

It's normal to fear change.
But do not let your fear hold you hostage.
Pack it up, carry it with you if you must.
Stare down your own darkness
and walk until you see the light.

CHAPTER 2

IT STARTS WITH YOU

WHILE THEIR HISTORY ISN'T WELL KNOWN TO MANY of us, spinsters are cultural icons. The term originates as early as the 1300s, referring to unmarried women who spun wool and earned their own living. By the 1800s, being a spinster was a secret source of pride: It was a privilege for a woman to remain unmarried in a time when the majority of women were economically bound to men.

Over time, in true patriarchal fashion, the word became distorted, and *spinster* carried a negative connotation. But in fact, these women who lived lives of autonomy and independence were *powerful*. It was the spinsters who, by fate or fortune, carved their own destiny and made the decision to remain single rather than marrying out of necessity, and if they did decide to wed, they would settle for nothing less than true, fulfilling partnership.

Today, many women still carry this patriarchal programming that our worth is tied up in our relationship status, but it simply isn't true. Having our identity wrapped up in whether or not we're in a romantic relationship is actually what distances us from having the depth of intimacy we crave on a soul level.

If we're afraid to be single because we believe it means something about our worth, then we're more likely to settle for crumbs, engage in self-sabotage, or self-abandon to hold on to a relationship that doesn't serve our highest potential. In my programs, I stress the importance of choosing the *inner work* with the correct intention. Doing the inner work cannot be centered around an external goal, like fixing another person, convincing someone to be more invested, or attracting a partner. It first and foremost must be rooted in self-devotion.

Conscious relationship is just as much about the relationship you have with yourself as it is about the relationship you have with others and the world around you. It isn't something you arrive at; it's a way of life.

It's okay if you also want to attract a partner, or heal a relationship with someone you care about, but you cannot expect to do either if you are swimming in an ocean of past hurts and resentments, anxious patterns, or fear of intimacy. As much as we all love shortcuts, there are none when it comes to healing our patterns. The only pathway to true, authentic love is to make the journey back toward ourselves, reclaim the parts we've dismissed or buried, and finally honor who we are in totality. We must take radical responsibility for our minds, emotions, and reality.

With feet planted firmly in who we are and what we want, we can then give voice to our desires and, if we choose, invite others to join us in a partnership that mirrors the rich, attuned relationship we've built within our own hearts.

GETTING IN RIGHT RELATIONSHIP WITH OURSELVES

The energy you carry matters. When someone is in self-rejection, we feel it. When someone is confident and comfortable with who they are, we can't help but feel drawn to them. And although it might not seem obvious at first, we know deep down when we or others are living in resistance to reality.

While the symptoms can look different for everyone, self-sabotaging patterns, letting people dictate our boundaries, not speaking up, feeling out of control, overthinking, ultra-independence, codependence, and emotional dysregulation are some of the primary indicators that we're out of alignment with our true nature. To be our most empowered selves, we need to learn how to trust ourselves and develop a spiritual foundation that guides us toward people and environments that are right for us.

Many of the obstacles we find ourselves facing in dating and love, like stagnant patterns where our relationships never seem to progress past a certain point, are due to holding back some part of ourselves. When we have a conscious relationship with self, we have the opportunity to become more accessible, alive, and genuinely expressed in each of our connections.

Building that relationship is the slow and gradual process of learning to witness your thoughts and reconnecting to your body and your emotions. It is bringing your needs, feelings, dreams, hidden or rejected parts, your light and your dark—everything that is a part of you—into awareness so that you can shift your energy from self-suppression to self-acceptance. When you do this, you are more likely to show up authentically, allowing others to see you and love you for who you are.

A Healthy Inner Relationship Starts With:

Building confidence and self-trust: Knowing yourself inside and out

Taking time for yourself: Being in nature, mindful of your breath, and tuning in to your body

Deepening in self-compassion: Meeting your walls and defenses with love and empathy

Giving your emotions a voice: Tuning in to the feeling underneath a feeling

Understanding your capacity: Knowing when it's time to take a break

Forgiving your past selves: Having compassion for mistakes and honoring your journey

Staying true to your values: Guiding your life from the truth of who you are

Expressing yourself: Having open and vulnerable conversations with people you care about

Asking for support: Leaning on a friend or speaking with a guide when you need help

SEVEN DATES TO BEGIN BUILDING
A MORE SECURE SELF

The more we get to know ourselves, the safer we feel in our own skin. This is why, to begin to build a sense of security and inner confidence, I encourage you to take yourself out on dates. Perhaps you already thoroughly enjoy your alone time; if so, then your mission is to get more intentional with how you spend that time. If spending time alone is hard for you, then making self-dating a regular practice can enhance your self-esteem and help you connect to yourself in new ways.

Whether it is a whole day, an afternoon, or thirty minutes, this time will help create a habit of nurturing your relationship to self. As you work your way through this book, choose one self-date, or more, to do each week—or feel free to come up with your own date ideas:

Take time to meditate, visualize, or practice breathwork.

Sensually and playfully dance to your favorite music.

Make yourself an herbal bath.
Afterward, oil your body and give yourself a massage.

Have an art night and practice intuitive painting or drawing.

Sign yourself up for a group class and get social.

Make yourself a nice dinner or go out to eat solo.

Take yourself on your ideal self-date.

LEARNING TO OBSERVE YOUR MIND

As we move deeper into this book, I'd like to invite you to practice observing your mind and being a witness to your thoughts, rather than being led by them. Observing your mind is the bridge to developing self-awareness.

The mind constantly produces millions of thoughts and stories. It makes meaning out of every experience we have and creates an automatic template for what to expect in the future. That's how our minds attempt to build safety, though it's a false sense of safety, because as long as we are letting the past inform our present, we're running on a predetermined script rather than letting life unfold naturally.

This is why you cannot believe every thought you have. Rather than immediately acting on a thought, you can slow down, take a breath, and ask yourself whether this thought feels true, whether it is based on a past experience, or whether it's simply meaningless! Then you can decide whether you want to respond to it or let it go. This self-observation is a vital aspect of the inner work and waking up to yourself. It is not coming from a place of judgment, criticism, or blame, but curiosity and compassion.

As you move through this book and learn to observe your mind, you'll notice that some of your thoughts are there to protect you. That's where the ego comes in. The ego acts as a defense mechanism to maintain your self-image and identity, to shelter you from the possibility of pain. But some of your self-protecting or defensive thoughts actually keep you separate from love and prevent you from being fully expressed. Sometimes your thoughts will tell you that *it's not safe to let love in*. Or that *it's not safe to be who you are*, or that you need to hold back your truth in order to win affection and approval. I want you to practice moving into a space of authenticity and vulnerability. We're going to take some risks in this program. It's important to be honest and put all of your cards on the table, to really let people see you for you.

There are times when we become stuck in a pattern, when we let our mind build a story, and we subconsciously seek to validate that story by acting out and cutting ourselves off from love. This is our mind trying to create a sense of safety through control. To release ourselves from this pattern, we must practice what's called *witness consciousness* (being a witness to our patterns) and surrender to the unknown. We can lovingly observe our thought patterns and habits as they arise and create distance from the negative reactions we've been conditioned to repeat. Virtually the only difference between a person who is self-aware and a person who is not is the ability to challenge the mind and to distinguish between one's thoughts and the truth.

Next time a negative thought, criticism, or judgment comes, take a deep breath and ask yourself:

What part of me is self-protecting with this judgment?
What part of me is trying to control things with this thought?
Is this thought coming from love or from fear?

If we do not learn to observe our minds, we end up believing every fear, every criticism, every judgment. The problems our mind creates become amplified until they begin to shape the way we experience the world, which, in some cases, can become debilitating or detrimental to our livelihood. Traumas and fears creep in and take up residence in our minds, and if we are not careful, we will begin to live from those places. The mind, if you let it, will tell you all sorts of lies about your worth or lovability. It takes practice to learn not to buy into the darkness. *The healing work is learning to observe our stories without attaching to them.*

YOUR INNER RELATIONSHIP IS THE FOUNDATION FOR ALL OTHER RELATIONSHIPS

Our past wounds and conditioned fear responses will rear their heads within our relationships, alerting us to what still needs our love and attention to heal. If all we have known is chaos, then our relationships will be chaotic. If all we've had modeled for us is deception, betrayal, or inconsistency, then our relationships will reflect the same. Every single one of us carries a pattern in relationship, and we will continue to act out those patterns in every interaction we have until we have done the healing work. The more grounded and centered we become, the closer we are to having relationships that reflect the home we've created within.

Our self-worth and self-esteem inform how we show up in *all* our relationships.

Building up your self-esteem and developing a relationship to the parts of yourself you've disowned is all for the purpose of integration. When you're integrated, you are the full, embodied expression of your whole, heart-centered you. This is cultivated by reclaiming your right to be vulnerable, sensitive, and attuned to your feelings.

Most of our relationship struggles stem from our insecurities, fear of using our voice, fear of being left, unloved, or alone. But imagine what may be possible in your relationships when you no longer need another person to fill a void or quiet a self-doubt, but rather, you seek a relationship for the sole purpose of finding someone to share love with in a reciprocal way. When we use our relationships as a source of approval, we can easily get lost in the other person. When we use relationships to give us the feelings we crave, we rely so much on the external that we no longer have any governance over our internal world. If we rely on a relationship as our main source of energy in the form of validation, or security, then the relationship becomes transactional. Chances are, we won't be able to fully recognize the red flags, state our boundaries, or make real positive change. *And this is why healthy, conscious love starts with you.*

We don't get to choose our attractions, and yet, our healing work can have a profound impact on who and what we're most drawn to. A large part of this is feeling secure in ourselves, so we can choose people, places, and environments that resonate with our highest self, rather than falling into the same situations time and time again.

HEALING OUR ATTRACTIONS

A woman once said to me, "I've got a broken picker." "A broken picker? What's that?" I asked. "It's when you have poor judgment for romantic partners and keep choosing the wrong ones," she replied. Since then, I've observed thousands of women who more or less say the same thing. Even though they crave a healthy and conscious relationship, they're still attracted to people who are either emotionally unavailable or utterly avoidant and totally unwilling to grow. On the other hand, when they do meet someone safe, they're bored. It's a frustrating cycle, and often results in feeling like they can't trust themselves when it comes to love. But we often choose what's familiar, even if that means staying in a place of discontentment.

You may be worried that you'll never be able to feel attracted to a partner who's actually healthy for you. I can relate, but I know you can do this. Throughout my twenties, I was consistently drawn to people who were, quite frankly, dangerous but alluring to me sexually. I found stability and safety boring and believed that I would have to sacrifice good sex and passion to be in a healthy, consistent relationship. My pattern was to go for a "bad boy," run the relationship into the ground, and then recover with a "nice guy." It wasn't until I met Ben in my thirties, after doing deep work on my childhood wounds, that I clearly saw my limiting beliefs around what I could have in love and realized that they were simply that: limiting beliefs, *not truths.* I've worked with so many women who say the same thing. They want it all—good sex, passion, chemistry, communication, and commitment. And I promise you, it's possible!

It's important to remember that just because you feel turned on doesn't mean you have to act on it. Just because you're attracted to someone doesn't mean you need to do anything about it. You don't have to have sex or pursue a relationship with anybody out of curiosity or feelings of passion, lust, or desire. Energy is just energy, and whatever you feel in your own body belongs to you. Instead of following every rush of attraction, you have the option to cultivate that energy and let it fuel your creativity and inner work instead.

Our attractions are not fixed. They reflect our inner relationship, which is constantly growing and changing. By creating more space for self-observation when we are feeling the energy of attraction, we can learn more about ourselves and take the first step in rewiring who we are drawn to.

ALIGNING WITH THE RIGHT RELATIONSHIP

When we enter the honeymoon phase of a relationship, which is a very passionate time, we may get excited and forget to qualify our potential partners. We might forget that we are still in an early stage of dating and we've yet to get to know the person—to have those deeper conversations about who we are and share what our dreams are, what our goals are, and what we want to give and receive in partnership.

Qualifying allows us to find out whether we actually align in partnership or whether it's just chemistry. There is a big difference between the two. We can feel a lot of sexual attraction and chemistry for a person yet not be compatible to move forward into deeper stages of partnership. Many of us are habitually seeking the rush of the honeymoon phase and mistakenly assume this high-intensity time is meant to last forever. But the honeymoon phase is meant to end—nature designed it this way. After all, you can't get much done, be responsible, or take care of a family if you're high on new love and having sex all day!

The beautiful thing is, there is so much more depth that can occur when we learn how to be in relationship as a spiritual practice—and over time, the gifts we receive are well beyond the chemical cocktail of pleasure and excitement we feel in the beginning. Part of aligning yourself for the type of relationship you desire is having a clear and direct line of communication between your heart, your body, and your mind so that you can bring consciousness to every step of the partnership.

On the other hand, if we're harboring a lot of past heartache, we might be guarded and struggle to let anyone in long enough to get beyond the initial dating stage. The inner work will help you be more open to love if you have been closed off or to slow down if you have a tendency to rush in, so that when you do meet a person that you can go deep with, you will be ready.

Having Self-Compassion Along the Way

Many of us get caught in a repetitive loop for a long time before we wake up and begin the healing journey, and this is nothing to be ashamed of. In fact, it makes perfect sense that we'd repeat the same patterns, because on some level, we're attempting to heal a wound or find resolution for something that happened in the past. As you uncover your patterns in love, rather than wondering why you didn't see it before, or wishing you could go back and change the past, you can choose to move forward with self-compassion and to find meaning in your life experiences.

THINGS TO REMEMBER

- Your relationship with yourself sets the foundation for all the relationships you have in your life.

- The inner work requires that you return to yourself and take radical responsibility for your mind, your emotions, and your reality.

- It's okay if you feel a bit disconnected from your authentic self right now. Be gentle and practice compassion.

- Rebuilding a relationship with yourself is a gradual process where you learn to witness your thoughts and reconnect to your body and emotions.

- Choosing to heal your relationship patterns is not about fixing yourself; it's about reclaiming your wholeness.

We spend so much time seeking strategies to feel better,
or to not feel so much.

What about simply being with whatever feeling is
present in you now?

Could you welcome it?

Could you tend to that feeling with love, the way you
would a small child or a precious thing?

Could you love your sadness and your grief in that way?

We label our feelings and limit ourselves from full expression.

Good, bad, positive, negative, too intense . . . which do
we embrace and which do we deny?

This is all a reflection of our capacity to voyage
into the unknown.

If we are willing to let go of the labels,
all that is left is energy.

CHAPTER 3

COMING HOME TO THE BODY'S WISDOM

WHETHER IT IS ACKNOWLEDGED OR NOT, WE ARE ALL energy-sensitive beings. When you walk into a room and something feels "off," that's your body responding to energy. When you sense excitement in the air, that is your body responding to energy. Yet we live in a culture that prioritizes logic and frames emotionality as weak, unstable, or untrustworthy. While this makes being at home in our body a challenge, it's possible to tap back into our sensitivity in a way that empowers and anchors us.

In chapter 2 we talked about learning to observe your mind. In this chapter, we'll carve a path to creating a conscious relationship with your body and your energetic environment, so that you may reconnect to your body's wisdom and grow your capacity to be with the full range of emotionality.

One of the major difficulties we may encounter while doing the inner work is how to self-soothe or process big emotions, energies, and sensations that arise along the way. If we are not in tune with our own body, we may react in ways that create further disconnection and breed shame and mistrust in ourselves. Disconnection from our body is often why we don't trust or deny our anger or sadness in the first place.

However, when we listen to our body and can sit with each of our emotions, we become more grounded, self-expressed, and confident. Being in your body is a key component of your healing, to returning to your truth. It allows you to be self-aware of your boundaries, your core values, and your intuition. As you navigate the rest of this book, and whenever things become difficult, you can center yourself by drawing on the practices and teachings found here.

WHY WE LEAVE OUR BODY

Many of us eject from our body very early on in life—often due to childhood trauma, abuse, or abandonment, or when we experience emotional neglect, which can happen even with loving parents. In response, binge eating, overexercising, food restricting, using substances, overanalyzing, reverting to logic over emotions, and avoiding intimacy are all ways we may attempt to numb ourselves and leave the body. So, when we feel stuck in a pattern and just can't seem to make the changes we want, our body likely needs more support to integrate our healing.

When we're children, our nervous system creates a map for how to respond to things like conflict, touch, connection, and feelings like anger, sadness, joy, pleasure, and so on. If something happens when we are young that causes our nervous system to freeze, fawn (people please), shut down, or go into fight-or-flight mode, our body may adapt and continue to respond into our adult lives as though the trauma or past experience is still happening. When we don't have the tools, time, or a safe place to heal, we can become trapped in this emotional loop until we have the stimulus our nervous system needs to release the trauma.

This can make it feel difficult and confusing to trust ourselves. We might believe that we can't "listen to our body" because we are unsure when it is responding to a past fear or an actual threat. But all sensations in our body are messages, and that is all you need to know to validate them. It doesn't matter whether the threat is real or perceived. If you don't feel safe, that is your body asking you to make a shift. Respond by getting yourself into a setting or an environment in which you can slowly and quietly listen to the message it is trying to give you.

We don't need to ignore, justify, or fix the sensations in our body. **Simply learning to be with the discomfort and letting our body move the way it wants to is healing.** Anytime we resist an emotion, we end up holding on to the discomfort longer, and we never complete the cycle. This can manifest as fatigue, physical pain, anxiety, and stress. If we listen, our bodies instinctively know how to release stored emotion. We may feel the urge to shake, jump, air-kick, or punch a pillow, go for a run, rub or massage our legs, or take a dunk in water. All of these actions are examples of our body's natural intelligence helping us process energy.

Many of us tend to live in our head more than in our body. Being in our body means having to feel, and that can be really scary when we're carrying inherited family trauma, along with our own fears, anxieties, and feelings of unworthiness. But when we are primarily in our heads and cut off from our body, we are also disconnected from our inner knowing. Not everything can be solved by thinking through it in profuse detail. Your body is a beautiful, intelligent source of wisdom for you. Being whole means your head, body, and heart are working in harmony to guide you. A deeply connected head, body, and heart is the brilliant result of an integrated and spiritual being.

BEING IN OUR HEADS LOOKS LIKE

- Immediately trying to make sense of a feeling
- Denying our emotional reality because it doesn't seem logical
- Using mind-centered language over body-centered language: "I think" vs. "I feel"
- Trying to talk ourselves out of feeling something
- Trying to justify why we're feeling an emotion
- Overexplaining our feelings
- Feeling "numb" or emotionally disconnected
- Viewing emotion and expressiveness as weak or humiliating
- Valuing composure over emotionality
- Focusing on the "facts" as if emotions have no value or purpose

BEING IN OUR BODY LOOKS LIKE

- Tuning inward and noticing an emotion as it arises and naming it: "I'm feeling sad, angry, joyful, nervous, etc."
- Locating and identifying the sensations in our body: "I feel tightness in my belly, my chest is feeling constricted, there is tension in my jaw."
- Using "I think" when you have a thought and "I feel" when you have an emotion, and knowing the difference

- Allowing your feelings and sensations to be there without needing to make sense of them
- Creating opportunities to move energy through your body (dance, screaming into a pillow, crying, deep breathing)

A HEAD, BODY, AND HEART CONNECTION IS

- Being able to differentiate between your thoughts, sensations, and feelings
- Knowing when you need time and space to process intense emotions before making a decision or initiating a conversation
- Trusting your body and exploring the messages it has for you without self-judgment
- Returning to your breath and noticing when your mind is making up a story or being self-critical
- Bringing presence into your body when you recognize you are overthinking or spiraling into fear and worry
- Self-soothing through breathwork, inner-child visualizing, or reaching out for support when you are overwhelmed
- Valuing both emotion and logic at different times
- Making space for magic, intuition, and unexplainable synchronicity in your life

THE ORIGIN OF OUR FALSE SELVES

As children, we are taught which emotions are safe and which will result in rejection, humiliation, ridicule, or feelings of helplessness. Many of us were punished for how we dealt with our emotions. We may have been left alone until we were "on our best behavior." As young humans, our brain and nervous system were still attuning to our caregivers. We needed them to help us through the big ups and downs, to teach us it was okay to feel, and to hold space for us when we were overwhelmed by our emotions.

Many of us didn't receive that, and so our adaptive responses found other ways to get the love and attention we needed, or sheltered us from the pain of not having our needs met by distancing from others. Early on in our first relationships with our caregivers, we begin to form our "adaptive selves" or our "false selves." Our "false selves" can also be called our "masks" or "shields." We put on masks as a response to trauma and feeling hurt or betrayed. We no longer show up as our "authentic self" because we've learned it isn't safe to do so.

Often, we carry these masks into adulthood, making it challenging to create healthy relationships. Instead, we may become guarded, defensive, or closed off, or hold back our truth. We might come off as aloof when, underneath, we crave love and attention. We might be outwardly loud and harsh when underneath we are quite sensitive and self-conscious. We can say or do things that don't feel authentic because we're worried about finding or keeping love.

THE SURVIVOR MASK

As a child, I was very sensitive and felt incredible waves of empathy and compassion in my heart. I wanted to make everyone near me feel loved, to heal every animal I met. Most of all, I wanted to save my mother from her pain.

When I was three years old, my mother would wake me up late at night and hold me while she cried and shared stories of her traumatic past. I remember how distraught she was as tears streamed down her face. I digested her stories of pain and abuse into my tiny body. I was confused and overwhelmed; I didn't understand why anyone would hurt someone they loved, like her mother had hurt her. I felt like it was my job to take care of her, to heal her suffering.

By the time I was twelve years old, I had endured physical and emotional abandonment on multiple occasions. I had experienced violation of my physical body in foster homes. I had watched my mother battle with addiction, depression, and suicide attempts, and I began my own habit of numbing with substances. The sensitive little girl in me became hardened and guarded as a protective mechanism. Nobody could get through my shields. I became angry and loud, mean and defensive. I wouldn't listen, and for the life of me, I couldn't receive love.

I wore the *survivor mask*, which is an archetype many of us step into when we come to believe we aren't safe in our vulnerability. The survivor mask protects us and gives off an air of ultra-independence, but ultimately, the "I don't need anyone but myself" mantra is a response to having been hurt or let down when we were most in need of support. *The survivor archetype has been conditioned to prioritize self-preservation at the cost of connection.*

I was aggressive and loud because too many times my sensitive nature and small stature had been taken advantage of. I wore a mask that told the world I didn't care. I cut myself off from my sensitivity completely and put on a show that I was untouchable, that no one could hurt me. But underneath my tough exterior I was in so much pain. I was lost, afraid, and desperate for validation and love.

School teachers and parents labeled me "the bad kid" because, where I grew up, only "bad kids" go to foster homes. Adults weren't there to protect me or keep me safe; they were there to vilify me. In my mind, no one was safe. It was me against the world.

So I ran away.

I fought.

I numbed my pain with drugs and alcohol.

I chased unavailable love from unsafe people.

My deepest awakening was catalyzed by my divorce. It was then that I finally recognized how much pain I had held in my body. How deeply I had self-abandoned. How sensitive I really was underneath it all.

Acknowledging our masks can be one of the most empowering stages in our healing. As we take responsibility for the ways we hide our true feelings or turn away from connection, we can shed those layers of protection and loosen our grip on our defenses. We can take baby steps toward showing our sensitivity until, eventually, we no longer need those masks at all.

Up to this point, your masks have served you well. In some cases, they may have even kept you alive. Now, you're building a new relationship to your emotional landscape in a way that allows you to stand in both your boundaries and your vulnerability.

WITNESSING YOUR EMOTIONS

There are no such things as good and bad feelings. Emotions are energy; they come, and they go. If we allow them in rather than resist them, they will pass quickly and transform. If we suppress or reject them, they can amplify in power and express in different ways: through constriction in the body and emotional dysregulation (feeling chaotic, being confused, disassociated, or unclear).

When we have an emotion, our initial instinct may be to try to "solve" it. Instead, we can learn to be present with our emotions without letting them dictate our behavior. While we can't control our feelings—nor should we try to—we can decide how we will react to them.

There are times when our emotions may be too overwhelming or intense to process in the moment, and that's perfectly okay. We don't have to get to the root of every emotion immediately (or ever, for that matter). We can put too much emphasis on dissecting an emotion to the point where we become obsessive.

Sometimes the best thing to do is get out of your head and move your body! Dancing, running, walking, or intuitive movement are all ways you can work with the energy in your body and shift your state naturally. Other times, there's a call to slowness, to rest and let your body process without your mind getting in the way. By doing this, you may actually feel more spaciousness to make a conscious decision or take action from a grounded place.

DEFAULTING TO ANGER OR SADNESS

In my experience working with hundreds of clients, I found there are usually two main modes of expression that women default to under stressful circumstances or in conflict: anger (fire) or sadness (water). Many of us either default to showing anger by being defensive or guarded or default to expressing sadness through grasping or guilt-tripping.

For those of us who lean toward the element of fire, our work is to practice bringing forward more water energy by letting down our walls and allowing ourselves to be seen in our vulnerability and tenderness. If our tendency is to block out anger and only allow tears or sadness, we might find ourselves unable to set firm boundaries, unconsciously guilting others rather than asking for what we need, or feeling helpless when it comes to our relational experiences. When we are low on fire and running on an excess of watery energy, we can get bogged down by the deep-dive emotions instead of taking action. **We want a healthy dance between the two, so that we can both allow ourselves to be vulnerable and speak up for ourselves or others when it matters most.**

When we've spent most of our lives cutting ourselves off from grief or rejecting our anger, it can be incredibly disorienting to feel these new sensations. Don't feel as though you need to rush yourself through any of these emotions.

If you're in a phase where anger is your dominant emotion, take the time to be with your anger in a way that gives you deeper access to your internal world. If sadness is your dominant emotion right now, learn from it, and let the emotion flow through you so that you can move beyond it. What's important to remember is that emotions are energy, and when we give that energy permission to pass through us, transformation occurs.

EMBRACING YOUR RELATIONSHIP TO ANGER

Most of us see anger as negative, even scary, because we are lacking a model of "healthy anger." We've come to think that anger is dangerous because throughout history, both in our own family systems and beyond them, anger either created separation through secret keeping and quiet betrayal, or it became violent and destructive. But healthy anger doesn't have to look like any of those things.

Anger is as sacred and valid as any other emotion. What hurts us is not that we have anger, but that we so often block it until it comes out sideways in the form of explosiveness, illness, or loss of self.

Anger is also the gatekeeper to other vulnerable feelings that lie below the surface: sadness, embarrassment, fear, and insecurity. While these are often painful emotions, each of these vulnerabilities can tell us something about ourselves. For example, fear can tell us when to be cautious or how attached we are to a certain outcome, and insecurity can reveal where we need to build self-trust.

More than anything, anger is an internal signal that lets us know when a boundary has been crossed. When wielded responsibly, our anger can fuel the fire we need to take action toward realigning with what feels right and true for us. But when anger owns us, instead of allowing it to empower us, we can become trapped in a brimming state of resentment. Feeling anger doesn't make you any less spiritual. Just like any other emotion—love, sadness, joy, rage—emotions are part of being a human on this planet.

If we repress our emotions, we automatically cut ourselves off from our fullest expression. We stunt and limit our creativity, our life force energy, our passion, and our wholeness. Anger is not the problem; rather, it is human reactivity and a lack of ownership that create pain. Embracing your own inner fire, witnessing anger in healthy ways, and learning impulse control are vital to becoming integrated and whole.

When you feel out of balance with your fire, you can bring in the water and earth elements to support you in grounding. Take a deep breath, go for a walk, go for a dip in the ocean or take a shower, take off your socks and shoes and feel your bare feet on the earth—return to your body. We all need time to come down from an emotional high. No one can think clearly or communicate well when they're triggered. If you're activated, take some space to be in your own energy and find your center.

WHEN YOU FEEL ANGER, ASK YOURSELF

- What doesn't feel okay for me in this situation?
- What do I need to feel safe, respected, and important?
- Am I holding back my truth?
- Do I need to remove my energy from this person or situation?
- Do I need to take action?
- Is there another feeling, besides anger, that I'm afraid to show?
- What emotions are underneath my anger?
- Do I truly need to protect myself right now, or are my defenses activated?
- Does this conflict or situation bring something up from the past?
- Is it time to explore the tenderness and vulnerability underneath my anger?

EMBRACING YOUR SADNESS

We live in an emotionally phobic culture, and just as anger is rejected, sadness too is often rejected and over-pathologized. Sadness is a necessary and vital part of our healing and recovery.

Moving through grief is a lost art. Instead, we live in an era where it is automatically viewed as a symptom of depression, rather than a time to honor and revere. We're often told that crying is weakness, that sadness is an unnecessary emotion. Especially in the world of New Age spirituality, there tends to be an overemphasis on "good feelings" while dismissing the value of going through the tunnel of anger, sadness, and grief in order to get to the other side. Bypassing these experiences is what leads to pathology; processing our emotions is what leads to healing. Sadness is not useless or senseless; it is purifying. Allow the tears to fall, honor the cleansing process, and be patient with yourself.

We often resist sadness, afraid that if we let ourselves feel it, we'll become stuck there, and there is some validity to that fear. Sadness is a watery emotion; it can feel stagnant, muddy, or over-whelmingly powerful. Think rushing rivers, waterfalls, and floods. It's a message for us to slow down and step into *being* rather than doing. However, if you notice sadness turning to bitterness or feel it's preventing you from connecting with others for a long period of time, then it has taken over and is becoming corrosive. In this case, movement is the medicine: dance, stretch, sing, make sounds. Make contact with your fire energy, and extend to others for connection and support.

WHEN YOU FEEL SADNESS, ASK YOURSELF

- How can I be tender toward myself right now?
- Where in my body do I feel sadness?
- Does my sadness have words?
- What am I in the process of cleansing?
- If I'm grasping, what is the deeper need I'm looking to get met?

- Is there a feeling, besides sadness, that I'm afraid to feel?
- Would it feel good to reach out for support?
- Is it time to shift my energy, or am I still in the process of clearing?

THE FOUR ELEMENTS OF EMOTIONAL INTEGRATION

Imagine that you are earth, fire, air, and water. Each of these elements makes up different aspects of our inner being, and each is important to the way we operate in our lives. We need a mixture of all four, even though we express as one or two of the elements more naturally—this is what makes us unique. However, when we lean too heavily toward one or two of the elements, we may be missing out on certain facets of life energy that we crave. For some people, that's self-esteem (earth) or sexual expression (fire); for others, it's creativity (air) or deep intimacy (water).

Most of us favor the elemental states that feel the most comfortable and lose touch with those that feel less familiar. Take fire, for example—the element that propels us to be piercing and truthful, to speak up when something is not okay. Many of us are disconnected from our fire. We fear that standing up for ourselves or setting a boundary might sever us from love. Or that if we don't take what we are given, we'll be left all alone with nothing. So, we settle for less, often making excuses for why it's acceptable. But the energy of fire, when wielded correctly, does not burn down relationships; rather, it fine-tunes our environment by being discerning with what we will and will not tolerate.

As you go through the descriptions of each element, can you identify which type you lean heavily toward? Once you determine which element you gravitate to, read the "growth opportunity" to learn how to embody other elements of your being.

EARTH: *grounded, ability to self-soothe, calm, rational, stubborn, present, gentle, nurturing, embodied, intuitive*

Earth types are naturally caring and gentle. Even though they may rely more on logic than emotions, their element also represents intuition, instinct, and renewal. Earth types orient toward a fixed reality, so change may bring up discomfort or stress. Earth types often carry a beautiful, grounded energy and make great listeners. They are also known to create nurturing environments that feel like home. Earth also governs security and self-confidence; in balance, earth is the source of high self-esteem and feeling at home in oneself.

Growth opportunity: When out of balance, earth types tend to worry, obsess, or be self-critical. To access their truth, intuition, and emotionality, they can lean into the element of water. Fire may also support an earth type in becoming more expressive and embodied. Air can help inspire earth to get out of their comfort zone and play more.

FIRE: *powerful, inspiring, hot-tempered, confident, sexual, intense, passionate, action-oriented, determined*

Fire types can be quick, passionate, bold, and alive in their communication. Fire as an element is transformative; it has the power to engulf or purify, depending on how it's directed. Because fire carries so much energy, it must be channeled in a positive direction. With nowhere to go, fire can be turned inward and translate to self-loathing. Fire types may be quick to anger and move quickly without realizing the impact their energy has on others. On the positive side, we can count on them to be authentically expressed and bring truth when necessary. Fire types are great starters in businesses and may often hold strong opinions about their beliefs and what they want. Fire provides inspiration to take action, create necessary change, and blaze a path forward.

Growth opportunity: When fire types are out of balance, what they need most is to slow down and allow themselves to soften, feel their feelings, and make space for vulnerability. Lean into the element of earth for grounding and compassion, water to tap into the emotional body, and air when it's time to envision a different future.

AIR: *etheric, thoughtful, dreamy, visionary, creative, social, friendly, mentally strong, intellectual, flighty*

Air has a quality of consistent movement. A nice gentle breeze on a warm day can remind us of the beauty of being alive. On a stormy day, air can be ungrounding, spinning us into chaos or even carrying us away. Air types can be visionaries, and dreamers. They are full of big ideas and future plans. Their gift is in sharing, writing, teaching, and delivering information. In relationships, air types may be perceived as aloof or have a challenge connecting deeply, even though they crave being seen and understood. Others may find them "hard to pin down" because they are always on the go either physically or energetically. Air is mostly associated with the mind and intellect. It is air that brings us insight, propels us to examine our beliefs, make plans, and communicate our ideas.

Growth opportunity: Because air types may be ungrounded at times, they need to draw upon the element of earth to anchor themselves in clarity, which can be especially helpful when making decisions or entering into or sustaining relationships. They should lean into water for emotional depth, and fire to help propel those big ideas into action.

WATER: *emotional, deep, soulful, intuitive, sensual, feminine, sensitive, psychic*

Water has long been used by various cultures throughout the world in ceremonial rituals for purification and cleansing. Herbal, flower or salt baths, water offerings, and water temples are seen as vital practice for clearing spiritual energies or illness. Because the expression of water comes in so many forms, there is an unpredictably to this element. Gentle yet fierce, life-giving yet potentially destructive. Water types are sensitive and dreamy souls, deep and wise with a desire to know people on an emotional level. Water types are often the ones that friends call for emotional support, but they may also be easily overwhelmed by emotion or empathy and need to set more boundaries.

Growth opportunity: Their gift is in seeing others deeply, though to harness this gift well they must embody self-awareness and avoid blaming others for their internal experience. Water types can call upon fire to draw a line in the sand when their energy is being taken advantage of or when they wish to bring forward more passion, joy, and play. They can call upon earth to stay tethered to reality and feel held when they are being pulled into the deep waters of emotion, and air to help them tap into creative solutions when they're bogged down or overwhelmed.

CREATING AN ALTAR TO
REPRESENT THE ELEMENTS

Creating an altar is a way for you to bring a heightened awareness to the energy you'd like to cultivate in your life. All that is required is an open heart and mind and a few objects that feel sacred to you. Find a place in your home that feels inviting and won't be disturbed by pets, children, or other creatures. Some people like to use a small table, a shelf, the top of their dresser, or even the base of their fireplace for their altar space. If you'd like, you can place a nice piece of fabric or cloth over it. The items on your altar can shift as you make your way through different phases in your own healing and growth and can also be respectfully gathered from nature—flowers, pine cones, stones, shells, leaves, moss, and even ocean water make beautiful altar items.

For your elemental altar, consider which element you feel is the most dominant in your life right now. If you lean toward fire or anger and struggle to be vulnerable, you may place a candle or other object on the altar that represents your fire or the reactive pattern you want to soften. Next to it, place a bowl or cup of water to represent your tenderness, depth, and vulnerability. Bring in a flower to represent softening, opening, and transformation. Make up your own configuration as a way to honor all sides of yourself and as an invitation to draw on other elements to help you find balance. Remember, all parts of you are lovable, and the very thing you're confronting may eventually be the energy you learn to channel as your gift.

NAVIGATING EMOTIONAL TRIGGERS

Our triggers are linked to our core emotional themes. Unhealed wounds are tender, and when we have an experience that activates a past hurt, we can become reactive or feel out of control before we even realize what's happening. A lot of times, we aren't consciously aware of what our triggers are, making the experience even more disorienting. Feeling excluded, abandoned, betrayed, forgotten, unimportant, controlled, rejected, or unwanted are common emotional triggers. Environments, smells, and images can also act as triggers. The smell of alcohol is a common one for those who grew up around alcohol abuse, or it can be the smell of a certain cologne or perfume, or a type of environment that reminds us of a place that harbors unfavorable memories.

Being triggered can cause us to retract or act out in ways that don't reflect our true nature, bringing up shame and self-rejection. But over time, we can build an internal base of safety that gives us space to pause and respond authentically, rather than just reacting. Feeling activated is uncomfortable; however, the solution isn't to craft ways to avoid ever confronting our triggers because this would likely mean avoiding relationships altogether.

Even the healthiest relationships have triggers, and this is not inherently an issue—it's how we deal with triggers that matters. If we react by projecting anger and blame at one another, then a container that could otherwise be a sacred space for healing quickly erodes into an unhealthy and unsafe environment. Similarly, we cannot shame ourselves into a healing moment; we need to bring self-compassion and curiosity to our process if we really want to understand ourselves better.

When we've spent time exploring our history and understanding our deepest needs for love and acceptance, we're much less likely to disown our emotions in moments of intensity and, instead, move toward an issue with vulnerability. **When self-awareness and willingness are present, our triggers become our teachers.** They show us where we have been wounded and invite us to honor the hurt, betrayal, and anger we may have never let ourselves feel at the time of the original injury.

Navigating emotional triggers requires us to bring mindfulness and presence to our body and mind. Once we've learned how to pause in an activated moment, we can choose to self-soothe rather than lash out, text our ex, call someone ten times during a conflict, chase unavailable partners, or make anxious demands of others. Most of us know how to distract ourselves from our emotional experiences, but learning to self-soothe, embrace our emotions, and move through them are skills that need to be developed.

The next time you feel triggered, find a quiet place and take a moment to yourself to do a self-soothing ritual or a somatic safety exercise. As you try different practices throughout this book, make a mental note of which ones helped you slow down in the moment, so that they can become a part of your personal tool kit.

SELF-SOOTHING PRACTICES

- Notice where you are, feel your feet on the ground, and count your breath.

- Step back from your thoughts and become the observer. Don't believe every thought you have.

- Tune in and name the sensations in your body. Find one place in your body that feels relaxed.

- Take a mental break from the situation and read a book for at least twenty minutes.

- Put your feet in a bowl of warm water or take a salt bath.

- Listen to a guided meditation or visualization.

Somatic Exercise: I Am Safe

This simple yet powerful somatic practice can help you regulate your nervous system and feel safe in your environment. It also serves as a reminder to come back to the present, helping your unconscious mind relax and know that you truly are safe (there's no tiger in the closet!).

1. Take a moment to feel your bum on the seat or your feet on the ground.

2. Notice your breath and take a few big exhales, letting out a sigh on the exhale.

3. Look up at the ceiling, then down at the floor.

4. Look behind you.

5. Notice the sensations in your body while scanning the room.

6. Notice any colors, shapes, or objects in the room.

7. While scanning, stay connected to your body.

8. Notice where you are, while remaining present with your breath and body sensations.

9. Say aloud or in your mind, "I am here, I am safe."

A RETURN TO NATURE:
SEASONS OF EMOTIONALITY

Coming home to ourselves means learning how to feel safe in our body once again. It means relearning how to navigate our big emotions with grace, reintegrating the parts of ourselves we've kept hidden, and unmasking *the authentic self*. Coming home to ourselves is a return to the wisdom of our own hearts and trust in our body, our intuition, and our worth. Regardless of relationship status, income level, or external achievement, you are deeply connected to love, nature, and Spirit.

Spending time in nature is one of the best ways to reconnect with your body's wisdom. When you are outside, take time to observe the cycles of nature. You are not so different from the plants or the trees. There is much to learn about yourself and your emotional world by seeing the ways you mirror nature.

The idea that we can think our way out of our patterns is a troubling message perpetuated by a hyper-success-focused culture. We pedestal action, completion, and goal-setting and have little reverence for the nuances of life. Being attuned to our nervous system, knowing what we need to feel safe, and learning to value our sensitivity requires that we step out of the dominant narrative, into a more rhythmic way of life. Slowing down to honor the rhythm of our cycles and seasons is an opportunity to return to a more integrated way of life, dancing in harmony with both solar and lunar (yin and yang) energies. Think of the phases you go through in life as akin to the seasons of the earth.

Nothing stays the same forever, and neither does your emotional landscape. While you're in this season of inner healing, you may find that you have entered a kind of "inner winter," a time of going within, where you need more quiet time, nourishment, and warmth. As your inner world shifts and changes, you may notice your needs and desires shift too.

When you're in a spring cycle, you may feel excited to start something new, take on a challenge, and meet new people. Similarly, in a summer cycle, you may have more creative energy and more capacity for social time, community, and relationship building. In a fall cycle, there is a shift inward again, a gearing down in preparation for letting go. All seasons are a beautiful opportunity to deepen your capacity to experience the full spectrum of your humanity. Consider what season you may be in now, and trust that wherever you find yourself is perfectly valid. Just like you cannot rush nature, you cannot rush your own process.

THINGS TO REMEMBER

- Emotions are energy, and they come and go.

- There are no "good" and "bad" feelings.

- You don't need to rush to change, fix, or solve your emotions.

- Emotions don't have to make sense to be valid.

- Not every emotion requires a response or an action; sometimes a little patience is all that's required.

- When your head and your heart are aligned, it's time to take action.

- Learning to separate emotions, sensations, and thoughts builds confidence.

- Self-soothing can be as simple as returning to your breath or feeling your feet on the ground.

- Allowing space for your emotional reality connects you to your intuition and core values.

- Nature is a beautiful teacher. Let the elements offer you wisdom and teach you about your inner emotional landscape.

- Bathe yourself in self-compassion as you come home to your body. You left for a reason, so return with gentleness and understanding.

Your inner child is home to all the
wonders of your innate essence.

To be whole, you must bring this joyful,
curious, playful, liberated, and expressive
part of yourself alive again.

CHAPTER 4

CONNECT WITH YOUR INNER CHILD

WHENEVER I'M OUT WALKING AROUND TOWN AND I see a stranger, I find myself trying to imagine who they were as a child. Were they silly, loud, and rambunctious, or quiet and shy? In the same way, anytime I see someone acting in self-destructive ways, or engaging in hurtful behavior, I remember that they, at one point, were someone's precious baby. Somewhere along the way, that innocent little child went through something that brought them to their current reality. When we see everyone, including ourselves, through this tender lens, it makes space for compassion, understanding, and a deeper spiritual access point to human connection.

We all have an inner child. This is the innocent, vulnerable "little you." Emotional rather than logical, this is the part of you that prefers to feel rather than think. While full of wonder, curiosity, and creativity, our inner child can also be a home to repressed traumas, fears, and painful memories—seemingly left in the past, but very much at the epicenter of our present day. As we grow into adulthood, we often become cut off from our inner child and, as a result, we are largely unaware of our emotional needs or why we act the way we do.

Even though we all grow up to be adults, many of us still relate to others through the lens of our child self. Emotional maturity is not a given with adulthood; it is learned through healthy modeling from our caregivers and other important adults in our lives and in receiving the loving guidance we all need to grow. But many of us were raised by parents who didn't entirely understand their own internal world, and thus were unable to support us in tending to ours.

How we behave in relationships reflects our emotional maturity. Long, drawn-out conflicts, game-playing, dramatic communication, and adult temper tantrums often occur with a hurt inner child at the helm. Many of us enter a relationship with a laundry list of expectations of our partners, some reasonable, and some unreasonable. How hungry our demands for attention and validation are reflect how nourished our inner child is at that time.

Inner child work, the work we will do together here, is a way for us to heal our unmet needs that follow us into our adult relationships. By contacting our inner child at various ages, we can tap back into the emotional experience we were having at that time and find new ways to nurture those parts of ourselves.

Keep in mind that it's virtually impossible for a parent to meet all of a child's needs. What one may perceive as a caring behavior, another may perceive as overbearing. Even if your parents were kind, loving caregivers, it's likely that you would still have unmet needs or parts of your childhood that carry an emotional charge. This process is not about blaming your parents or anyone outside of you; it's about developing a direct line of communication between little you and adult you so that you can embody emotional maturity and wisdom in your relationships. This is how we step into the *integrated adult* within each of us.

Accountable for our emotional reality, our integrated adult *also* has the capacity to consider someone else's emotional reality. It means being deeply connected to our emotions, noticing our body's sensations, and observing our thoughts, so that we can identify and communicate big emotions. Our integrated adult is what allows us to remain true to ourselves during conflict and act from a grounded place—rather than responding with anger, overreaction, or shutting down. It is how we live in the present, no longer ruled by our past influences or experiences.

We can only become this integrated version of ourselves when we have learned to welcome all of the rejected qualities of our inner child and witness them lovingly rather than try to eradicate or suppress them. It means accepting the neediness, the impatience, the jealousy, *all of it.* This is how we become whole, forge an unbreakable relationship to ourselves, and set the foundation for healthy love.

As you begin to open the lines of communication with your inner child, you will certainly find new joy, innocence, and creativity; you may also recognize ways they have led you to act out in your adult life. I want you to remember that while you are doing this work, anything you may discover about yourself is valuable. You are not alone if you have acted in ways that you're not proud of within your relationships. There is absolutely nothing to be ashamed or embarrassed about. If you have chased love, pushed it away, or tested it until it broke, then your inner child may have been crying out for your love and attention.

This is an invitation to begin to listen to that inner voice. You will find strength, clarity, joy, healing, liberation, and so much more when you do. Bring with you compassion, gentleness, and acceptance as you take these next steps in reclaiming the self.

THE GIFT OF THE
CHILD ARCHETYPE

If you've ever spent time with children, or maybe you have children yourself, then you know that they don't tend to hold back in any fashion. If they're happy, they're happy; if they're sad, they're sad; if they're angry, well, they'll let you know and they don't care who's watching!

With maturity, we learn to calibrate our emotional expression and take time and place into consideration. If we were fully expressed with our emotions all of the time, we'd be having fits in the breakroom or dancing on tables at work. Instead of integrating our inner child, we tend to leave them behind because somewhere along the way we were taught that it's unsafe to be vulnerable, that our emotions aren't welcome, or that it's not okay to express pure joy. While some filters are necessary for our everyday lives (like choosing *not* to have a tantrum at work), we ultimately go too far and lose connection with that unfiltered part of ourselves. We guard our hearts, hold back our truth, disguise hurt feelings, and go on the attack instead of being vulnerable. Awakening our inner child can help us unwind these self-destructive patterns and find peace.

AWAKENING YOUR INNER CHILD
ALLOWS YOU TO

- Tap into more joy and awe every day
- Access the full spectrum of your emotional reality
- Ignite your curious, creative, and playful side
- Have an open mind
- Be in total self-expression
- Embrace your dreams and desires

REFLECTING ON
YOUR CHILDHOOD

Think back to when you were small; do you remember your childhood? Some people don't, and if that's you, don't worry, you can still connect with and heal the relationship to your inner child. But if you do have memories, what was it like for you growing up? Were your parents emotionally available or distant? Were your own big emotions validated and held, or punished and shamed? What was the emotional climate in your household growing up—was there joy and celebration, open and honest conversation about feelings? Or was your family conditioned to sweep things under the rug, see emotions as problems to be fixed, and keep secrets? Did you feel celebrated or criticized?

As a very young child, I didn't feel there was a safe space for my emotions. My mother didn't understand emotionality or her role as the parent and mine as the child; she took everything I said and did very personally. I remember having a conversation with her a few years ago while we were driving, and she mentioned that we got into a big fight when I was two years old. "We got into a big fight when I was two years old?" I asked. How was that possible, I was just a baby! "We got into a big screaming match," she said. I asked her if she understood that as the parent, it was her role to hold space and help me learn how to process my emotions, and she said, "I had no idea! I always thought it was about me!"

I valued her honesty and bravery in admitting that she didn't have the emotional language to parent me as a child. Our conversation highlighted for me how little guidance I had received in learning how to validate my emotions or ask for help when I needed it.

A parent's emotionally phobic behavior is not a reflection of how much they love their child, but rather a symptom of their own disconnection and the lack of nurturance they received when they were children themselves. Parents who were raised in an emotionally unsafe household tend to pass down a similar emotional environment to their children. Even so, it's not the ruptures in connection between parent and child that wound us long term, but the lack of repair—acknowledgment or an apology—that keeps us from healing.

Emotional or psychological injury at a young age is the origin of the *wounded inner child*. When we've grown up disconnected from our emotions, we may find it difficult to trust others, to ask for or receive support, or to show our vulnerability out of fear that we'll be rejected. We may self-abandon and accept less than our worth just to fill the void, or take over from a past caregiver who was highly critical by continuing to demean or put ourselves down. This is the root of the wounded inner child. Healing the wounded inner child, and strengthening new pathways, requires practice and a willingness to meet new parts of yourself with grace.

When we discover how to step into our integrated adult, we are able to give and receive love, and ask for support, while maintaining appropriate boundaries. We are also able to tend to ourselves in moments of heightened stress, grief, or conflict rather than pushing emotions away or projecting them onto others.

SIGNS OF A WOUNDED INNER CHILD

- A deep-seated belief that you are broken
- Fear of abandonment and loss of love
- Feeling insecure or not good enough
- Low self-esteem and negative self-talk

- Loss of self in an attempt to gain approval from others
- Fear of setting boundaries or saying "no"
- Seeking instant gratification through substances, shopping, distraction, and procrastination

BRING YOUR INNER CHILD INTO CONSCIOUSNESS

When we are cut off from the needs and the voice of our inner child, we may unknowingly operate in relationships from the lens of our child self. We may see others as a source of the energy, love, nurturance, protection, and acceptance that our child self craves. Unconsciously, we can carry weighted expectations that our partners will be everything we never got from our parents as children. While relationships can be healing and deeply fulfilling, they cannot fulfill all of the missing pieces from our childhood or change the past. So, when our partners do not live up to these expectations, we relive the pain and may act out unconsciously in destructive ways, totally unaware that our wounded inner child is the one wreaking havoc.

This doesn't mean we need to shut down our inner child; in fact, it's quite the opposite. It's the rejection of our wounded inner child that causes chaos. To show up more authentically in our relationships, we need to bring our inner child into consciousness, listen to their fears, their dreams, and desires, uncover what past traumas or memories require healing, and take them under our wing. **When a healthy dialogue has formed between our inner child and our adult self, the result is the integrated adult.**

At the same time, just like we would listen to a child but not let them drive our car, we want to acknowledge our own inner child, but not let them drive our life. When our wounded inner child becomes the driver of our lives, we may behave in immature ways within our relationships, having tantrums, blaming, reacting impulsively, lying, making unfair demands, or being unwilling to compromise. We may also internalize all of the criticism or neglect we experienced as little ones and become our own worst enemy. Tending to your inner child energetically is about drawing on the wisdom of your adult self and listening empathically to their voice that wants to be heard, and then responding with maturity. It is becoming the source of protection and nurturing love that is sourced from deep within your very own being—from your inner mother and father.

Most of us would likely never dream of speaking to an innocent child the way we speak to ourselves in our own head or of ignoring a little being who is in emotional suffering. So why do we try to push down our own needs and ignore our own inner child when they need us most? Reconnecting to the child within is a chance to change how you talk to yourself and give yourself the kindness and empathy you deserve.

THE WOUNDED INNER CHILD IN RELATIONSHIP

- Struggles to understand emotions and express them
- Expects their partner to know what they want without saying anything
- Gives the silent treatment when hurt or upset instead of speaking up
- Disregards their partner's experience and expects them to hold space unconditionally
- Yells, screams, attacks, or throws a tantrum when upset
- Is self-centered during conflict and struggles to consider alternative realities

THE INTEGRATED ADULT IN RELATIONSHIP

- Connects to body sensations and emotions
- Identifies their needs and clearly communicates
- Asks clearly for what they want
- Remains true to self even in conflict
- Sets and honors their boundaries
- Gives space to their inner child to have big feelings
- Practices self-love and self-care

THE ANXIOUS-AVOIDANT DANCE

Two months into my relationship with Ben, we started doing group Tantra and shadow work training together. We would spend anywhere from three to nine hours per week practicing, and we were on the path to being in a "conscious relationship." But even though we had the desire and the willingness, for the most part, we were both not as emotionally mature as we thought, and this was reflected when we were in conflict. We were two people deeply committed to the inner work, and Ben is also a counselor, yet here we were doing the *anxious-avoidant dance* with one another!

It looked something like this: We'd have a conflict, we'd both get emotionally dysregulated, and things would escalate. Ben would pull away, and I'd lean in harder and make demands that we have a clearing or process the conflict right then and there. I was certain that I was the conscious one and he was avoidant, and that it was on him to fix this problem we were having. Naturally, since I was the one ready and available to process things, I also believed that I saw the situation clearly, and because of this belief, I could easily tell him all of the ways he was going about it wrong. Very little of my psychoanalysis was spent on my *own* inward process.

After doing this dance for about a year and a half, we were coming to a major tipping point. I was exhausted with feeling emotionally abandoned and rejected when I needed him most, and he was exhausted with feeling like a failure. Neither of us was winning, and we both wanted to find a way out. One day, it dawned on me that this entire time, I had been trying to fix the pattern by trying to *fix him*. Rather than considering why Ben felt the need to pull away or what might be occurring for him when he would get tired and shut down or leave the house and go to the gym, I was convinced it was because he didn't care, had no feelings, or simply wasn't ready to "do the work." I was pretty high and mighty!

When I approached him to talk about the pattern we were in, he was probably expecting another monologue about what he could do to show up, but instead, I apologized to him for being so self-centered in our conflicts. I told him that I felt I saw the pattern clearly, but I also realized that I had been placing all of the responsibility on him instead of taking ownership over my own emotions and learning how to self-soothe. "From now on, if you're not able to hold space for me during a conflict, I'm going to go into the other room and hold space for my inner child," I said. At this time, we were in the power-struggle phase of our relationship, so another conflict arrived quickly and I took the opportunity to practice self-soothing. Instead of making demands of Ben or grasping, I informed him that I was going to go process my emotions.

Hands placed on my heart and belly, I closed my eyes and took long, deep breaths and affirmed that it was safe to feel all of the intensity that was arising in my body. I noticed fear, panic, discomfort, and then surrender as I continued to move toward the pain rather than run from it. As I let my inner child speak, she told me how afraid she was to be alone, and I saw that this whole time, I had been ignoring my inner work by focusing on trying to fix my partner.

What was once almost a deal-breaker in our relationship transformed into a gift. Ben's pulling away gave me the opportunity to get to know my inner child and her needs once again, to regain security within myself and learn how to self-soothe when needed. If he had come rushing in every time we had a conflict and I was triggered, I wouldn't have had such an opportunity to build a more secure and healthy attachment style within myself.

As a result of taking responsibility for my own emotions and giving Ben the space he needed, his energy shifted too, and he began moving toward me and feeling ready to resolve conflict sooner. In the present, we don't play the anxious-avoidant dance anymore. But it took us a long time to get to this point, and it didn't happen through force; it happened through surrender. Both of us turned inward first, before we were ready to turn toward each other in a mature and conscious way.

I share this story in almost all of my workshops and online courses because the majority of folks I work with have experienced this anxious-avoidant dance in one way or another. Learning about our attachment styles can be a powerful way to understand ourselves and the dynamics we find ourselves in. Every step we take to feel at home in our body frees up energy to relax into love rather than run from it.

At the root of our being, we are designed to attach to others. Healthy attachment looks like learning how to give and receive love without abandoning ourselves. When our attachment needs—things like physical touch, a consistent loving presence from a caretaker, emotional attunement, nurturance, and boundaries—weren't met early in life, we may still grapple with loss of self. This translates into feeling absorbed by another person any time strong feelings are involved (this applies to family, friends, and romantic partners alike), or we experience a fear of abandonment. Or we may have grown accustomed to gut reactions of chasing and anxiously pursuing, shutting down during conflict, or avoiding intimacy altogether. These all stem from a childhood that did not provide a healthy and secure base to lead from relationally. However, attachment styles are not fixed but fluid, and with willingness, we can all move into secure attachment.

WHY LEARN TO SELF-SOOTHE?

Developing the capacity to self-soothe is not about pushing others away or being ultra-independent. In fact, learning how to take ownership for our internal reality is what empowers us to know what we need and ask for support from people who can really be there for us.

When we are in a panic and desperately need someone to save us from our big emotions, we lose ourselves. That's when we're more likely to push people away or pursue unavailable or unsafe people. Self-soothing is important for all adults. It's not our partner's job to rescue us from our feelings, and if we don't know how to navigate what arises inside of us, we'll project, blame, grasp, chase, or pursue our partner unfairly.

Self-soothing is empowering because it gives us the ability to understand ourselves—so that we know when to hold ourselves and when to get support. Slowing down, listening to our body, and communicating with our inner child allows us to pause and react in a mature way. And being responsible for our energy and emotions means that we can return to ourself instead of ejecting from our body when things get too intense.

Healing Your Inner Child Meditation

The next time you find yourself feeling insecure, anxious, overwhelmed, sad, shut down, or triggered, find a quiet place and take yourself through this visualization. A guided audio version of my Healing Your Inner Child Meditation is also available to download on SheleanaAiyana.com.

1. Lie on your bed with your eyes closed and place your hands on your belly and heart. Take a few deep breaths, and breathe out any tension or tightness in your body. Visualize light coming into your body, and begin to relax.

2. Notice the sensations in your body—notice your emotions, and give them a name. See whether you can also locate where the emotion is in your body.

3. Now, visualize yourself with your inner child. Notice the environment that you and your child self are in together. Are you in your old family home? Are you in your bedroom? Are you somewhere in nature?

4. Say hello to your inner child and ask them what they are feeling, and then just listen. Maybe they have a lot to say, and maybe they are quiet. If they are quiet, simply be with them and hold them with love. Invite your inner child to sit in your lap or snuggle with you. Let them choose.

5. Let your inner child know that you are the adult and you're going to keep them safe. Let them know it's okay to feel. Tell them you're not going anywhere and you will always take care of them, listen to them, and give them space to express themselves.

6. Take a moment to share kind and loving words with your inner child. If you're not sure what to say, try some of these

affirmations: I'm here for you, all of you is welcome here, I'm going to protect you, I love you.

7. Give your inner child a gift, like a teddy bear, to symbolize the connection you now have. Visualize a warm embrace with your inner child, and breathe together. Imagine your inner child dissolving into you, as you become one. Stay with this feeling as you continue to breathe.

8. Notice the sensations in your body, and notice what you are feeling now. Observe the places in your body that feel more relaxed and safe than before. Take a few more deep breaths, wiggle your toes, and stretch your limbs.

9. Open your eyes and look around the room. Attune to your surroundings and say, "I'm safe here."

Come back to this process any time you need to self-soothe. When you deny or repress your emotions, your inner child suffers. As an adult, you can now begin to "parent" your own inner child by being self-loving and compassionate when emotions arise. Inner child work is not something we do to completion; it is a lifelong practice of being tender and nurturing with the most vulnerable parts of our being. Going within and paying attention to visions and images we receive can also connect us more deeply to Spirit. Meditation, music, and time in nature are the antidote to our feelings of isolation. We can be alone yet connected, and it is when we are in the deep that we meet new parts of ourselves.

INNER CHILD RITUALS

Connecting with your inner child can be a fluid part of your daily practice. It is a beautiful way to regularly tap into your right brain and unleash more of your creative, intuitive, and visionary qualities. If you feel any resistance to this work, it might be exactly what you need. Sometimes we experience resistance because we're afraid of what we might feel in the process, or we're not comfortable being the child when for most of our lives we've felt more like the parent.

Creating a nourishing and spiritually connected relationship with your inner child through ritual is a healing balm to the heart and soul, a journey back to your innocence. Time and time again, this work has brought me from a place of fear and separateness to a place of genuine warmth and oneness with Spirit. The following rituals and meditations are the practices I have used throughout the years in my own personal healing, and I'm so happy share them with you now.

To start, you may wish to set aside time at least once a week to do one of the following rituals, and then build up to a daily practice. As your relationship with your inner child develops, you'll find that you feel connected to this part of yourself all the time. When challenges arise in your life and your child-self tendencies surface, you'll have the awareness to listen attentively and then respond from the wisdom of your adult self.

- Do a body scan—tune in to physical sensations.
- Close your eyes, visualize "little you," and form a dialogue. Ask questions like, "What are you feeling?" and "What do you need right now?"
- Draw a picture, paint, or make art that reflects your inner child. Imperfection is perfection!
- Nurture your creativity and do something you loved when you were small.
- Write a letter to your inner child from the energy of your wise inner parent.
- Use mantras like "You're safe," and "I am here to take care of you."

An Altar to Celebrate Your Inner Child

Choose a childhood photo of yourself to place on your altar with your favorite flower and a small candle. If you don't have a photo of yourself as a child, you can choose an image that represents your child self. Next, gather a few items that represent your inner child, like a teddy bear, favorite childhood candy, or special object. These items should be very specific to who you were as a child and spark a sense of aliveness, energy, and remembrance. When you look at your altar, spend a moment filling your heart up with love and acceptance for your inner child. Then choose one way that you'd like to tap into your inner parent and nurture your inner child that day.

THINGS TO REMEMBER

- Your inner child is meant to be nurtured and integrated, not rejected or shunned.

- A healthy connection with your inner child will help you be more authentic.

- By healing your inner child, you are remembering your oneness with spirit and nature.

- This work is about learning to listen to your inner child attentively, and then respond from your wise inner adult.

- Your inner child is also home to your joy, creativity, and ability to celebrate life. Let yourself play, laugh, and have fun.

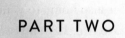

PART TWO

HEAL
YOUR PAST

My child, you were never abandoned. I have always been here, loving you unconditionally. You simply forgot that you are one with the universe. Remember who you are and come home. Wrap yourself in the divine embrace of the moon and the stars. Everything about you is perfect.

—SPIRIT

CHAPTER 5

HEALING THE ABANDONMENT WOUND

WHAT DRIVES US TO ANXIOUSLY CHASE PEOPLE OR push someone we have just met to commit? What's behind the intense fear of rejection, the gut-wrenching feeling of being unwanted, or the impulse to prove ourselves when a person signals they are emotionally unavailable? Why is it that so many of us feel more turned on by someone who isn't healthy for us than by someone with whom we could cocreate a lasting partnership?

These are the questions so many of my readers and clients want answers to, and they are the force behind the relationship patterns many of us are seeking to end.

At the root of nearly every human being's quest for relationship is a deep desire to feel wanted, seen, heard, and understood. This desire is amplified when there is a past trauma or an experience of being unwanted, unseen, neglected, or misunderstood. What's often left in the wake of these past hurts is an *abandonment wound*.

The abandonment wound is so powerful that it can permeate every area of our lives, dictating our behavior at work, at home with our families, and in our friendships and romantic relationships.

When the abandonment wound is active and unhealed, building a secure and loving relationship may feel downright impossible.

Having an abandonment wound is not purely a mental construct or a mind-set; it is woven into the nervous system, where we form habitual and adaptive responses to ensure survival. When left unchecked, it may form *maladaptive responses*—avoidance, withdrawing, passive aggression, uncontrolled anger, self-abandonment, and more. These are the kinds of responses that hold us back from forming healthy connections with others. Leaving before being left, never letting your guard down, and anxiously chasing unavailable people are the echoes of an abandonment wound.

EMOTIONAL ABANDONMENT

I once worked with a woman named Jade who would get incredibly triggered any time her partner needed space in a conflict and she had no idea why. For the most part, her relationship with her parents was good. She couldn't think of anything that would cause such a stir in her, but when we talked more about her childhood, she shared that whenever she had a big emotion, or expressed her anger, she was immediately sent to her room alone. She remembered feeling overwhelmed, scared, and totally abandoned in those moments. Suddenly she connected the dots and found her core emotional theme. How she felt back then was exactly how she had been feeling in her relationship.

This initiated a big "aha moment" for her. Jade saw how her partner needing space in a conflict brought her back to that time and caused her to act out from her wound, making accusations or blanket statements that pushed her partner further away. Moving forward, Jade decided to practice taking a pause when she felt like lashing out and to empathize with the part of her that was afraid of being abandoned. She knew change wasn't going to happen overnight, but she was committed to developing more trust and honoring her partner's boundaries in a conflict.

When I talk to people about the abandonment wound, they presume it means literal abandonment by their parents. They may have all the signs and symptoms of an active abandonment wound but not feel justified if they felt they "grew up in a normal family" or had both parents present. But these wounds can form when we feel emotionally abandoned and in many other experiences that are common to an overwhelming majority of humans on this planet. Some spiritual traditions even believe that the original abandonment wound occurs when we are first birthed into this world and the umbilical cord is cut.

It's almost inevitable that most people enter adulthood with some sort of an abandonment wound. And while some of us have stories that seem extreme, and some that may seem mild, there is no need to compare histories to validate our experience. Each of our stories might be different, but the wound is the same. The beauty of healing the abandonment wound is moving beyond the idea that we are broken or incomplete and remembering our connection to nature, and to the divine love that exists all around and within us.

ABANDONMENT WOUNDS CAN FORM WHEN

- A parent leaves or passes away
- A parent is physically there, but emotionally unavailable
- A parent is physically absent (never having met a parent, being adopted)

- We had a health complication as a child or at birth that required surgery, hospitalization, or separation from a parent
- A parent ignores, punishes, or denies our emotional experience
- A parent is gone for a while (on vacation, a work trip, etc.) and we don't understand their absence
- Our parents go through a contentious divorce, remarriage, or there is infidelity
- A parent is chronically ill and unavailable to tend to our emotional and physical needs
- We're sent away when we don't want to go (grandparents' house, summer camp, etc.)
- In our adult lives someone close to us leaves abruptly, betrays us, or dies

AN ACTIVATED ABANDONMENT WOUND

Our abandonment wound can be activated in minor ways any time we're interacting with people who mean a lot to us. On a subtle level, there can be a sense that we're never safe or that at any point a good thing is going to be ripped away from us. It's the experience of constantly waiting for the other shoe to drop.

Many of my clients have described the bodily sensation of the abandonment wound activating as a hot, intense, panicky feeling, or like they want to jump out of their own skin. This is where creating a daily ritual of attuning to your body and practicing a gentle return to center is especially helpful.

SYMPTOMS OF AN ACTIVATED
ABANDONMENT WOUND

- Feeling threatened when someone you love shares negative feedback or criticism

- People pleasing to keep love

- Lacking the ability to let other people have their own experience

- Controlling other people

- Feeling anxious about being left, assuming the worst

- Catastrophizing even in minor conflicts

- Forming codependent alliances, choosing to only trust one person and demonizing the rest

- Reverting to the child self during conflict

- Avoiding hard conversations, setting boundaries, or sharing feelings that might "rock the boat"

- Chasing commitment from emotionally unsafe or unavailable people

- Rapidly moving toward new partners before getting to know them

- Punishing partners with the silent treatment rather than communicating clearly

- Pushing love away, struggling to receive help, affection, or gifts

- Feeling turned on or excited by rejection

- Losing yourself in other people and abandoning your own hobbies, goals, or friendships in favor of a new love interest

- Feeling insecure and riddled with self-doubt

- Holding on to an ex-partner with an intensity that can feel all-consuming

SELF-ABANDONMENT

Fear of abandonment can ironically lead to self-abandonment. When we're preoccupied with the fear of being left or unloved by another, we may negate our own needs, deny our reality, and suppress our emotional experience to keep the peace. But there are great consequences when we self-abandon.

At the center of all people-pleasing behavior is a belief that we must contort ourselves to fit into other people's lives. The reality is, we must create spaciousness within our own lives for the right people to come or go based on alignment. Self-abandonment happens when we have a need or desire and don't speak up out of fear that we'll be rejected. It's in the moments where we drop everything when someone calls even when we had plans, or when we stop nurturing friendships because we are caught up in a romantic love interest. Ending this cycle of self-abandonment begins as we peel back the layers of our own fear of abandonment and claim ourselves—quirks and all.

This also means taking risks, expressing ourselves, setting boundaries when something doesn't feel good, and taking a stand on the things that matter to us. We're not willing to do these things if our main priority is to keep the love at all costs. *In order to build a truly conscious relationship, we have to be willing to let ourselves be seen in the truth of who we are, with clear ownership of our desires.*

SIGNS OF SELF-ABANDONMENT

- A pattern of falling in love rapidly with new people
- Dropping everything for a person we're attracted to
- Ignoring red flags or obvious signs of disinterest
- Pretending to be someone we're not to win approval
- Spending all our time with a new love interest, sidelining close friends
- Using social media to spy on an ex, or their new partner
- Breaking boundaries we set for ourselves
- Using alcohol or other substances to avoid uncomfortable feelings
- Saying yes when we want to say no
- Worrying more about pleasing others than honoring ourselves

DATING AND ACCEPTING THE UNKNOWN

The dating world can be confusing and intimidating. Which app do you use? When should you text them back? How soon should you be getting back out there after a breakup or a divorce? When can you have the "relationship talk"?

In my workshops, I often see clients do the inner work, get super clear on their values and what they want, but find that they're still in a big rush to secure a committed relationship. There's nothing wrong with wanting a relationship, but there are subtle ways that the anxiety of being abandoned can still have a grip on our relationship patterns, and one of them is racing through the dating phase into commitment without an exploration phase. Instead of asking ourselves questions like, "Do I like this person for who they are? Do I feel safe with this person? Are our core values aligned?" the focus instead falls on urgent matters of the wound: *Am I being chosen by this person?*

Impatience is usually the drive to get out of an uncomfortable feeling—and when it comes to dating, we're talking about the discomfort of not knowing what comes next, whether this is the person we're going to end up with, or whether they're just a stop along the way. I see folks apply a lot of pressure very early on in a relationship and they feel devastated when the person they are pursuing begins to distance themselves. When we lean in too far, this force of energy can naturally cause someone to move away rather than toward us.

You have a right to check in on where the other person is at and what they're looking for, but sometimes we get confused about what this really means. Some of the people in my program will meet a person, date for a few weeks, and then expect the other person to be 100 percent in and ready to go deep, but it takes time to know someone and have the conversations required to decide whether you're aligned to go further.

Remember that everyone moves at their own pace and it's often unrealistic to expect that other people operate just like you do on every level (mentally, emotionally, spiritually). You can honor your boundaries and be clear with what you desire, while also making room for their reality too. There is a big difference between someone telling you flat out they don't want a relationship and someone moving slowly and taking the time to get to know you.

With an abandonment wound, the process of dating without knowing the outcome can feel excruciating. But moving too fast into a relationship before you've had time to explore can also back-fire. While there is no set time, one to three months generally gives a couple space to get to know each other, and to ask important questions, so that both can gauge their level of desire to go deeper. Some folks who have children and are considering a blended family may require a lot more time than this, as the decision to merge impacts more than just the people entering the partnership.

There are also many folks who enter the dating scene while their abandonment wound or heartbreak is still fresh, and this can muddy the waters in the dating pool. It's not that we need to be perfectly healed before we go out and meet new people, but when our anxiety is high and our confidence is low, we may become exter-nally focused and fixate on being wanted rather than paying atten-tion to what is going on inside of us. Instead, we want to wait until that burning sensation of urgency and the anxiety have passed, un-til we are ready to accept the great unknowns of dating, love, and relationships and move forward from a calm and grounded place, anchored in our authenticity.

REJECTION AND THE ABANDONMENT WOUND

Letting go of someone who has rejected us can feel debilitating. When someone walks away or leaves us, we're left with so much emotion to sort through. Our abandonment wound can become activated, unearthing our deepest fears of being too much, or not enough. This may cause us to cling too tightly to someone who doesn't want to be with us. But just because we feel deeply attached to someone doesn't mean they are the person we were truly meant to be with.

When we just can't seem to let go, thinking of them con-stantly or desperately strategizing how to "win them back," there's something else going on beneath the surface. It is our inner child that needs tending in these moments, so we can step in with our loving inner parent and take care of our hearts rather than self-abandon. If we tune in to our inner child when we are experiencing rejection, we might find they are feeling:

Scared

Hurt

Abandoned

Unsafe

Rejected

Not enough

Unseen

Unimportant

Forgotten

When a small child is feeling those things, what do they need most? Safety, security, reassurance, and protection. When our wounds are triggered, we naturally believe the person we're fixated on is the solution to our pain, and that if only they would return to us, they could make us feel good again.

The truth is, someone who doesn't want to be in your life cannot make you feel safe. You can learn to love yourself whole, to become the safety and stability you've been externally seeking. Instead of spending all your energy wishing for them to return, devote yourself to coming home to yourself. Healthy love isn't a game. You don't have to "work" to be loved. You are innately lovable and worthy, just by being you.

THE THREE ABANDONMENT ARCHETYPES

The abandonment wound often manifests itself in three ways in our relationships. While some of us anxiously chase love and commitment, some of us fear it and choose the path of ultra-independence, while others become over-givers. Here are three abandonment archetypes.

The Love Chaser

Love chasers often hold on to romantic fantasies and "imagination-ships," hoping there is more to the relationship than there really is. They may actively pursue unavailable or emotionally avoidant partners and see their efforts as virtuous, believing that they can help this person "heal" or open their hearts. In some cases, a love chaser may be obsessive and pursue someone well after the door has been closed. Love chasers may find themselves haunted by dreams of a person for a very long time, struggle to get the person out of their mind, or secretly check the person's social media. This archetype is also prone to falling quickly for a person and racing toward commitment. Their work is to practice being in the body, slowing down, communicating more directly, and honoring themselves by continuing to engage in their friendships, hobbies, and other commitments during the honeymoon phase, rather than shape-shifting for their new love interest.

The Ultra-Independent

This type finds safety in leaving before being left, or keeping people at enough distance so as to not let themselves get hurt. The ultra-independent prides themselves on their strength and ability to do it all on their own. Often, this archetype feels lonely and unseen, but struggles to accept help, direction, or support. One of the biggest struggles for this archetype is that they don't let people in very easily, so when they finally do, it's much harder to let go of a relationship, even if it is unhealthy. Ultra-independent types are often very private and don't let many people see their true emotions or inner world, and this can often lead to codependent or imbalanced relationships. The ultra-independent has to slowly let down their walls. The key is *slowly*, so they don't overwhelm their nervous system. Asking for help and being willing to "not always have it together" is a helpful practice to soften the beliefs that they have to do it all on their own. Leaning into friendships that feel safe and nourishing is a great way to practice relationship skills!

The Over-Giver

This archetype feels an intense need to be loved and validated and often carries an unconscious belief that they have to work to earn love. The over-giver may have learned early on that they get more attention or acceptance when they do well or perform in some way, and so this energy may translate into self-abandonment and giving beyond their energetic capacity. Over-givers may pour themselves out until they are drained and resentful. One of the greatest challenges for the over-giver is that they may give with a load of expectations that they don't voice, while simultaneously struggling to speak their own needs for fear of being rejected. The over-giver has to learn how to prioritize themselves, create balance when it comes to how much energy they give, and communicate more directly about what they want and need. They may also need to become more aware of the impact their energy has on others and recognize when they need to rein it in and give space.

We may find ourselves embodying one or all of these archetypes at different times throughout our lives. Sometimes, the pattern shifts depending on who we're with. In my case, I realized that my boundary-setting game was strong in virtually every other area of my life, except with close female friendships. Because my deepest wounding occurred with my mother, who struggled with depression, whenever a female friend was depressed or going through a difficult time, all of my boundary setting and awareness would go out the window and I'd unconsciously start playing the over-giver again.

Be patient with yourself if you find that you keep falling back into one of these archetypes. Untangling yourself from what's familiar is a slow process. But no matter which archetype you find yourself playing out in relationships, your pathway to integration and healing is the same.

HEALING THE ABANDONMENT WOUND

By accepting the full spectrum of who we are, we create an opening for the right people to enter our lives and love us fully. If we are fighting to be chosen, we are living in service to our pain. As we heal, we develop the trust and capacity to create a new destiny, embodied in our highest expression. We cultivate the courage to set firm boundaries and ask the important questions that give people an opportunity to show us who they are.

Healing the abandonment wound isn't about erasing our past. Healing does not mean getting rid of, but rather, "being with." When we are unaware of our wound, it has the power to create mayhem in our lives. When we are aware of and tending to our wound, it has the ability to bring us deeper into ourselves.

Your wound is not who you are. It is simply an area where you will be more sensitive, and through time and patience, an area where you have the potential to gather wisdom, empathy, and understanding for yourself and other beings. I don't believe our wounds are our broken parts, even though they feel that way. The gift our pain offers us is a passageway to uncover our hidden potential. Healing the abandonment wound does not come with a formula. Healing happens in connection to the self, and in slowly reminding our nervous system that we are safe.

These are some of the practices that can help you on the journey to healing your abandonment wound.

Rebuild a Connection with Your Inner Child

As you learned in chapter 4, the bond you build with your inner child provides a strong and secure base from which to lead your life. Connecting with your inner child empowers you to step into a more mature and self-aware version of yourself. When you feel panic, dread, anxiety, or uncertainty, you can tune inward and ask your inner child to communicate all of their feelings, thoughts, and fears. Remember that the abandonment wound is often an echo of a past hurt—it is the lingering pain of the nurturance you never received, the attention you craved, the love you never got. When this wound is activated, tap into your protective inner parent to set boundaries and offer yourself healing. Your inner child is always there, waiting to be seen, heard, loved, and accepted.

Let Yourself Feel

Resistance to feeling creates a block in life energy. Practice allowing your feelings and sensations in; as they arise, bring curiosity without judgment to your experience. Many of us learned to deny or suppress our feelings to avoid embarrassment, ridicule, or overwhelm. But emotional energy needs to be felt to process and move through the body. The more you hold on, the heavier it gets. Consider each emotional experience as a cleansing of your heart and mind.

Do Somatic Work (Get into Your Body!)

Healing happens by reinhabiting your body and returning to self-trust. In addition to guided therapy like somatic experiencing work, there are a host of simple practices that will help you learn to listen to and trust your body. Take time throughout the day to pause, notice your breath, and name the sensations you're feeling. When you're holding on to pain and trauma, the inclination is often to stop moving. Nature walks, dance, trauma-informed yoga, and self-massage help nurture you back into relationship with your body.

Learn How to Set and Maintain Boundaries

Every time you honor your boundaries—whether it is a boundary you've set with yourself or someone else—you are actively doing the work to heal your abandonment wound. Remember, self-abandonment is one of the side effects of having an abandonment wound. When your wound is activated, you are craving attention, love, and validation, and you may do anything to get it, including abandoning your own needs or stretching your boundaries too thin. Small acts of staying true to your own energetic, emotional, or physical boundaries will help you build strength and courage in creating the life you truly want. We'll dive more into boundaries in chapter 12.

Ask for Help

Asking for help from others creates new opportunities for people to show up for you, and for your brain and nervous system to integrate a new reality. If asking for help feels challenging, or if you feel resistance reading this, chances are this is your growth edge. When I was younger, I never asked for help. In an attempt to impress others and receive validation, I'd go out of my way to do everything myself, all from scratch. I even used to hand-crack my peppercorns when cooking dinner! Asking for help can feel incredibly vulnerable for an ultra-independent person, but as human beings, we build intimacy by showing up for each other when things are tough. Give others a chance to see your heart and be there for you.

Let Love In

If you've been taught that you're only lovable in a certain emotional state (most likely happy and agreeable), then your work is to bring new sides of yourself and your vulnerability to a partner or close friend. *Learning how to trust others is intrinsically linked to learning how to trust that you're worthy of receiving love and support.* It's also important to be discerning with who you bring your vulnerability to. Choose people who have demonstrated they are emotionally safe. A safe person is someone who can listen without judgment, offer reflections rooted in empathy, and who won't seek to fix your problems or try to talk you out of your feelings.

Stay Committed to Your Interests, Hobbies, and Values

Do you work around the other person's availability as soon as you enter a relationship? Do you scrap your plans last minute and drop everything when they call? Sometimes we leap toward someone without giving them space to move toward us and show their interest. Remember the relationship you have to *yourself* needs to be home base. Stay committed to the things you care about and don't make the relationship your entire world or identity. Instead, find things to do with friends, join in a group activity, and show up for the commitments you've made. Not only does this anchor you to your own core, but it also makes you more magnetic because you are demonstrating your worth through your actions.

THINGS TO REMEMBER

- Having an abandonment wound does not mean that you are broken.

- Your abandonment wound points to the most vulnerable and tender parts of your inner child.

- An abandonment wound can happen even if you had a loving family.

- An abandonment wound can occur when your emotional needs weren't met, even if your parents were physically present.

- Healing your abandonment wound does not mean that you'll forget about the past or stop desiring love, closeness, or reassurance. It means you will no longer be ruled by your pain.

- While healing your abandonment wound, it's important to practice being attuned to your body and naming your emotions.

- No one else is responsible for healing this wound. Someone can give you all the love in the world, but you also have to do the work to let that love in.

- When your abandonment wound is triggered, practice inner child work, self-soothing, asking for help, and being in connection with others.

The beauty of healing the mother–father wound is learning to accept the limitations of our parents. Moving beyond the endless search for others to fulfill our longing for safety, love, and stability, we learn to find them within ourselves and in nature.

CHAPTER 6

DIVINE MOTHER AND FATHER ENERGY

THE MOTHER AND FATHER RELATIONSHIP IS COMPLEX and unique to each one of us. No matter how we grew up and whether our parents were present emotionally, physically, or neither, the relationship we developed to our parents in childhood plays a part in the relationship experiences we will have throughout our lives. Most of the heartache we endure within our mother or father wounding is the result of their own unprocessed pain and unhealed trauma. Trauma is inherited and it replicates through generations. But as much as we can pass down our traumas, we can also pass down our wisdom and our gifts.

The root origin of the word *heal* is "to make whole." While many of us may not have the opportunity to have a deep spiritual or transformative conversation with our parents in this lifetime, each and every one of us has the capacity to end the negative cycles of our own family history and find wholeness again through our relationship to Spirit.

Through this part of the inner work, you're going to remember how to connect to the divine energy of mother and father that is universal and not limited to the humans who brought you into this world. On my own healing path, I found great solace in my connection to nature. During moments of despair and grief as I uncovered the depths of my own parental wounding, it was the moon and the stars, the trees and the river that held me close and reminded me that I am never alone—and neither are you. We are a part of this great universe, connected to every living being, plant, and animal that calls this place home. We are all related.

YOUR RELATIONSHIP WITH YOUR MOTHER AND FATHER

If you have a good relationship with your parents, you might think you don't need to explore this aspect of the inner work, but I encourage you to go in with curiosity. You may discover something subtle that makes a huge difference in your present-day relationships. If you are adopted, you may want to explore your relationship to both your biological parents and your adoptive parents. If you've never met your biological parents, you can still investigate this relationship on an energetic level, which is something I had to do in my relationship to a father I had never met or even seen a photo of.

If one or both of your parents was absent, abusive, unwell, or passed away, you may find it helpful to return often to the inner child meditation in chapter 4. It may also be important for you to seek support as you unpack your history. Remember that it's okay to go slowly, or simply let these words stir in you until you are ready to take the next step. There's no rush to go there if you're not ready.

If you are a parent yourself, you may be tempted to make this chapter about how you show up as a parent, rather than tuning in to your own relationship with your parents. The very fact that you are holding this book in your hands is a testament to the kind of parent you are. Trust that every ounce of energy you redirect back toward your own healing process is a gift to your child, no matter their age or what you have been through together.

While we do have an impact on our children, we cannot entirely control how they turn out or who they become. They come into this life with their own unique soul path to live out and we are simply stewards, here to watch over and care for them as they find their own way. It's impossible to be everything for our children, and when we truly recognize this, we can release ourselves from the heavy burden of expectations to do it perfectly and instead be authentic in how we relate to our kin. Right now, allow yourself to get messy, to focus on yourself—this is where healing our relationships begins.

WHAT OUR PARENTS TAUGHT US ABOUT LOVE

As small children, we see our parents as gods. They are our protectors, providers, nurturers, and guides. Our survival quite literally depends on them caring for us. The very first relationship we have in life with our parents is where we learn everything we know about love, connection, and safety.

If our first years in this world were spent in the loving and secure arms of an emotionally safe parent, this impacts the rest of our lives and how safe we feel in the world. Alternatively, if they were wrought with disconnection, or lack of nurturance, this too will show up in our present-day relationships.

The mother–father wound is felt as the missing sense of protection, love, and acceptance we did not receive from our parents. While the abandonment wound develops more from the sense of being left alone with our hurt, the mother–father wound carries the tenderness we may feel around having missed out on receiving nurturance and consistent care from our parents. There are myriad early experiences that can cause a mother–father wound, such as growing up in an environment where parents fought a lot; enduring an emotionally or physically abusive household; being punished when expressing big emotions like anger, jealousy, or sadness; having an emotionally shut-down parent who was unable to show affection or provide support; being adopted; or losing a parent to addiction or illness.

If we didn't have our needs met as children, we may carry this wound into our adult lives and seek resolution from our romantic relationships. And while partnership certainly offers us a chance to heal our past, we must also recognize that our partners and friends are not responsible for the actions of those who came before them.

HOW MOTHER–FATHER WOUNDS PRESENT IN ROMANTIC RELATIONSHIPS

- Anxious-avoidant dynamic
- Chasing unavailable love or emotionally avoidant people
- Rescuing people, having poor boundaries
- People pleasing
- Codependence
- Low self-esteem
- Trust issues
- Jealousy
- Self-sabotage (affairs, distancing)
- Feeling insecure in relationships
- Being addicted to chaos and turbulence
- Freezing, shutting down, or avoiding conflict
- Abandonment wounding

WOUNDED MOTHER AND FATHER ARCHETYPES

Most of us grew up experiencing aspects of the following archetypes in a mother, father, or caregiver. The point of this is not to criticize or blame your parents but simply to notice what resonates for you, and to better understand what you were taught about love. With this information, you are invited to bring into awareness inherited patterns and any resentments you may be holding on to so that, eventually, you can learn to release them and put the cycle to rest.

The Absent Parent

The absent parent is either rarely or never physically present, or is physically there but emotionally numb, making them unable to be a nurturing force. One example of this archetype can appear in homes where there is also an abusive or addicted parent, and the other caregiver doesn't protect the children or remove them from the environment. Even though there may be valid reasons why that wasn't possible, through the interpretation of the child self, this feels like abandonment. Those who grew up with the experience of an absent parent may have a hard time receiving nurturance and support, or they may find they are attracted to unavailable types and get caught up in trying to win love.

The Abusive Parent

The abusive parent is the expression of control and domination, a gross misuse of power over those who are unable to defend themselves. The abusive parent often has their own traumatic and abusive past and continues to play out that harm in their own family. Those who grew up experiencing an abusive parent may have a hard time trusting love in relationships because closeness feels like it can lead to pain. There can also be a deep sense of internal shame and feeling disconnected from Spirit—a sense of feeling forgotten.

The Withholding Parent

The withholding parent is physically present but emotionally absent. They may be there in body, but are cut off from their heart and unable to offer empathy, connection, guidance, or emotional leadership to their child. Those who grew up experiencing a withholding parent may have learned to disconnect from their feelings and senses and overly rely on logic.

The Addicted Parent

Preoccupied with their addiction to work, money, sex, or substances, the addicted parent's energy is scattered, evasive, self-centered, and unreachable. The signature qualities of this archetype are physical or emotional absence, selfishness, and role reversals. Those who grew up experiencing the addicted parent may have had to become the parent when they were really the child. As adults, they might repeat patterns of rescuing and caretaking in their romantic relationships. They may also struggle with low-self esteem and following through on the things that matter to them.

The Helpless Parent

Unable to properly care for themselves or their children, the helpless parent may lean on their children for emotional support and unfairly burden them with the weight of their own past wounds and traumas. The helpless parent archetype can also express itself through seeking relationship with people who will "rescue them," but this often comes at a cost, as these rescuers will most often be unintegrated themselves and can be abusive, controlling, or dismissive. Those who grew up experiencing a helpless parent may develop rescuer tendencies and can also become avoidant in relationships because they fear enmeshment with others.

The Rejecting Parent

The rejecting parent is often one who experienced abuse or rejection from their own parents. This may have caused them to shut down, be unable to access their own emotions, and thus reject the emotions of their child. The rejecting parent sees their child's big emotions as a problem or "bad," and is unable to provide support or guidance in how to move through them. Rather, they punish the child, isolate them, or, in extreme cases, abandon them. Those who grew up experiencing a rejecting parent may struggle with confidence and self-esteem and get triggered by the feeling of being misunderstood.

The Guilt-Tripper

The guilt-tripper gets compliance from their children through guilt and shame tactics. The energy of this archetype can also express through manipulation, breeding resentment and mistrust. It can be challenging to set boundaries with a guilt tripper. They may respond to requests for growth with comments like, "I can't do anything right," or "You're trying to change who I am." But there's a difference between trying to change who a person is and having standards for how we choose to interact. Those who grew up with the guilt-tripper archetype may develop a lack of boundaries or wall off from others to avoid "emotional manipulation." They may struggle to trust others, be sensitive to feeling controlled, or become defensive during conflict.

The Dream Crusher

The dream crusher is highly critical, doubting, and cynical. This is the parent who will tell you all of the reasons it can't be done, or all the negatives of a decision or dream you have. It's important to remember that dream crushers are often wired for negativity because that was the experience they had with their own parents, and sometimes they actually believe they are helping you by giving you the "facts." When you share your dreams or plans with a dream crusher, do so only when you are confident in your path and you aren't looking for encouragement—you won't find it here. Those who grew up with this archetype may feel like they always have to prove themselves or earn love, and they may struggle to slow down or rest. If you have a dream crusher in your family system, you may need to set boundaries around communication and criticism.

PERMISSION TO FEEL, TO SET BOUNDARIES

You can simultaneously hold immense love and fierce boundaries with your parent. If you feel anger toward them for the way they've shown up (or failed to show up) for you, honor that. We cannot bypass our anger and skip to love and light—it doesn't work that way. *You have full permission to feel how you feel.* It's vital to take the time to process your anger before you try and rush yourself into a space of compassion.

Anna was a twenty-seven-year-old woman in one of my programs who spent years tending to her mother, who struggled with her emotional and mental health. On many occasions, Anna's mother crossed her boundaries in extreme ways to the point of getting physical with her. As time went on, Anna began to unwind from her own trauma and realized she desperately needed distance from her mother. When her mother lashed out again, she finally spoke up and told her she would be taking space and that she would no longer stick around when conflict escalated. Suddenly, her mother was motivated to change, but Anna wasn't overjoyed. "My mom is finally in therapy," she told me. "She called and wanted my praise, but in my head all I was thinking was, 'This is the absolute bare minimum you could do. Get yourself together!'" She explained that right then, she just couldn't access compassion for her mother.

I nodded in agreement; I had been in her shoes. There was a time in my own life where I was so angry at my mother that I would end almost all of our conversations by hanging up on her. She wasn't the one to help me work through that anger, and most of the time, our parents simply can't be those people.

In many cases, trying to process our pain with our parents can be counterproductive. Unless you have a shared language, your parents will likely struggle to understand where you're coming from, and it's possible that the conversation will only lead to more frustration and hurt feelings. But we all need to find a safe space to navigate that anger and discern how to proceed with the relationship. Often sharing your internal process is best reserved for a trusted guide or therapist, someone who won't take things personally and can simply validate your experience and make useful reflections that can further guide you along the way.

Many people feel guilty for saying they felt abandoned or betrayed by their parents, especially when on paper their parents did the "right things," like put a roof over their heads and food on the table. But we need more than just food and shelter to form healthy attachments, and it's okay to acknowledge your personal reality.

Making sense of some of your patterns by going within and acknowledging the ways you felt unheard, unseen, misunderstood, or abandoned is not about parent blaming; it's about coming to terms with your anger, resentment, or grief so that you are free—free to write a new story, free to see your parents as innocent, free to choose a new pathway forward. When we deny our emotional reality to protect others, the pattern will emerge elsewhere, often in our romantic relationships. We cannot outrun unfinished business, so the only way to be free is to feel what is there to be felt, care for the child within, and make peace with our past.

Our heavy emotions can also be a guide for when we need to set boundaries with the people in our lives. As with Anna, if family members are unable or unwilling to engage with us on a healthy level, then we need to find the strength to distance ourselves and take the time we need to regain clarity. And when we do feel ready to engage with them again, we have the strength to set the terms.

WHEN A PARENT DENIES OUR REALITY

When I was twenty-one, I began to see the world differently. I learned about observing my mind, challenging my thoughts, and rewiring my belief systems. With the excitement of my newfound spirituality, I became determined to help my mom wake up too. I spent a lot of time trying to teach her things, to point out how wrong her reality was, to help her heal faster. Underneath it all, what I really wanted was a connection with her. I wanted her to heal so that I could experience that loving nurturance from a parent that I never received. This only led to more misunderstanding and confusion.

In my late twenties, when I spoke to my mother about how I had grown up in and out of foster homes from the age of three to sixteen years old, she denied this reality. I was shocked and confused. After we hung up the phone, I wrote out a timeline of all the homes I bounced around to, just to find my center after feeling so gaslit by our conversation.

After that experience, I chose to do my healing work without her involvement. It wasn't until I began to learn about my own defenses, my ego, my wounded inner child, and the part of me that was still grieving all that I had endured as a child that the healing really began. And as I healed, I began to soften. I began to understand that my mother's shields from the past were a form of protection from her own unspeakable trauma and her internal guilt surrounding my childhood. It was a way to distance herself from the immense grief she felt at not being able to have a do-over as a parent.

From that place, I was brought into deep compassion and reverence for the fact that she had survived so much. I no longer wished to force her into the work, because I recognized that our paths were different. She was doing her best, and she simply wasn't ready or resourced to open up her past; trying to force that on anyone isn't kind. In place of my desperate attempts to "fix" my mother, I dropped into admiration for all that she had overcome. As I loosened my grip, she eventually became more curious and open.

In any family system there is usually one outlier. The outlier is the one who wakes up and commits to breaking cycles of inherited family trauma, dysfunction, or chaos. Chances are if you're reading this, in your family system, the outlier is you. There can be a sense of loneliness for the outlier, as we move through the grief that surfaces any time we step outside of a relational pattern and shake things up. This loneliness and the gravity of what we are learning can drive us to want to share what we've discovered with our parents or family members. We might think it's up to us to help them see where they went wrong, or for them to reconcile the ways in which we felt unloved, rejected, or unsafe with them. But the truth is, this likely won't turn out the way you hope. You can find completion with these feelings without bringing them into your process. There is so much pressure on parents that the guilt of feeling like a failure can often be too much to bear.

People have healing realizations in their own timing in accordance with their path, and it's not our job to get them there. And the reality is, we don't have the power to do so. Part of our inner work is to accept others for who they are, set boundaries that keep us safe, and make room to meet people where they are. When we wake up, not everyone will understand. They might feel threatened by it, they might feel scared, or they might deny our past experiences to keep themselves safe from uncomfortable feelings.

If your parents invalidate or dismiss your experience, it's because they either can't confront that part of their own past and the guilt that comes along with it, or they don't have the emotional capacity to be curious with you. If they are guarding a sense of shame, the result is defensiveness or denial. Please know that it's not your fault if you've experienced this.

When we feel an overwhelming desire to help people with their inner work, we are being invited to look closely at what we might be avoiding in ourselves. When we want to wake someone up, we are essentially hoping to change them in some way, and we often want to change someone when there's something in it for us, such as more acknowledgment, love, approval, recognition, connection, and intimacy. Our needs are worthy of being met, but not everyone will be receptive to our invitations for growth and deeper intimacy. Fortunately, we do not need anyone to change in order to love ourselves, and we don't need to make anyone else do the work to begin doing our own.

Since that experience all those years ago, my mother has been able to have some of the hard conversations with me. She apologized for denying my reality and acknowledged my experience. But it didn't come on my timeline, and that's where I was able to see the gift she gave me. When she denied my reality back then, I had to make a choice to go inward and validate myself without seeking it externally. I also had the chance to deepen in my connection to Divine Mother energy that felt so potent to me anytime I was in the forest or sitting in ceremony, and to see her innocence above all else. Sometimes, we don't get what we're looking for on our own timing because there's a deeper transformation possible when we have no choice but to give ourselves what we're craving from others.

SELF-ACCEPTANCE AND THE MOTHER–FATHER WOUND

We mirror our parents' movements, behavior patterns, and expressions. If we have fond memories of our childhood and a good relationship with our parents, this isn't much of an issue. However, if our memories of our parents are coupled with pain, judgment, or disgust, the place we find ourselves in is self-rejection and shame. We are all like our parents in some ways, and being able to acknowledge this makes way for deeper self-acceptance.

Before healing my mother wound, I would look in the mirror and feel a pit in my stomach when I saw her features reflected back at me. I have her eyes and nose, and that terrified me. Not because I find my mother unattractive to look at—she's adorable. It was because looking at my own reflection reminded me of her, and I had yet to find forgiveness for her.

As I began to delve deeper into myself, I was able to access new feelings for my mother. Slowly, I began to notice all of the ways I was like my mother, and rather than pushing that awareness away or feeling that pit in my stomach, there was a warmth. I started to see the qualities I had inherited from her that I loved and admired.

Once I was willing to face the darkness of my own self-rejection and the rejection of my mother, I was able to access a deeper sense of self-love and integration.

From my mother, I learned not to sweat the small stuff. To be generous, to play and be silly. To celebrate for no reason. To believe in myself, and to persevere. When I was finally done with being angry at her for all the things she wasn't, I was able to celebrate all of the things she was.

Bringing into awareness your parents' traits, characteristics, and patterns is the first step to seeing how your relationship to your mother and father expresses in your present day—specifically, how you view yourself, how willing you are to embody certain aspects of your nature, and what you reject most in yourself and others.

When you are feeling grounded and open, find a quiet place, light a candle, and follow these journaling prompts.

Mother

Something I dislike about my mother is:

Qualities of my mother that I reject in myself are:

Something I always wanted from my mother is:

Qualities of my mother that I like in myself are:

Father

Something I dislike about my father is:

Qualities of my father that I reject in myself are:

Something I always wanted from my father is:

Qualities of my father that I like in myself are:

Things to Look for in Your Journaling Process

The traits you dislike or reject about your parents may also be the traits you struggle to accept in yourself. The key here is to practice becoming more aware of when those qualities present in you, such as a tendency for blaming or guilt-tripping, and instead of pushing it down, just be with it. You'll notice these behaviors more with a new awareness around them, and this gives you the power to shift.

Tune in to your body as you are going through this journaling process. Sometimes if you see something in your parents that you really dislike, you will fight your instincts and swing to the opposite end of the pendulum. This indicates an area where you can stretch. One example of this is: "My mother was an artist, and I hated my mother, so I never lean into the instinct I have to draw and paint." This is the wound holding you back from expressing your gifts and stepping into your fullest expression. Leaning into the wound means embracing the ways we are like our parents, even if they challenged us. By doing this, we make room for our own integration, no longer trying to be more like, or not at all like, our parents and focusing simply on being ourselves.

Notice the things you said you wanted from a caregiver that you never received. Do you see any remnants of this in your romantic relationships? Do you consistently choose partners who also activate that old, familiar longing inside of you? Is it possible that the love you want is right in front of you but you're not able to see it through your current lens? If this resonates, this is an invitation to connect to your inner resources through self-soothing, inner child work, and nature.

Recognizing the ways you are like your parents is an opportunity to deepen in self-acceptance and self-love. Notice the positive things you may have inherited from your parents too; this is an opening to soften.

SEEING OUR PARENTS' INNOCENCE

In my early-twenties, I learned about the potent healing plant medicine from the Amazon called ayahuasca.* I felt drawn to work with it, but at the same time I was terrified. I knew I had so much healing work to do before I would be ready to embark down that path. Over the years there was a quiet whisper inside of me that pulled me closer to sitting in ceremony, but I waited and continued to do my inner work and learn from other plant medicines. When I was going through my divorce, a message dropped in loud and clear: *It's time for your soul to be stripped bare.* I knew it was time to chip away at the walls around my heart. It was time to strip my ego away and find out what was waiting for me on the other side.

Some time after this intuitive experience, I met Ben. He had begun his own journey working with ayahuasca and invited me to join him and his trusted curandero. So, after six months into our partnership, off we went to our first ceremony as a couple.

In those first three nights, I faced my mother wound head-on. I lay in the dark ceremony space and suddenly the medicine hit me. I was thrust into a swampy green jungle, and it was loud and disorienting.

---

* While ayahuasca has been a vital part of my own story, in no way am I recommending you work with ayahuasca unless you are certain this path is calling you, and you have a trusted and integral guide. Plant medicines like ayahuasca require that we work with them with the utmost respect and humility. I never recommend going to Peru and sitting with a shaman who's advertising at a market or with a local healer who has not trained under a lineage. Spiritual tourism is harmful, not only for the vine herself, but also for the people of the traditional cultures and places in which she grows. Please be deeply mindful and intentional if you choose to work with this medicine and know that the plant medicine path is not a fast track or a quick fix. In many ways, it is more intensified and can even be overwhelming. There is medicine in gentleness too, so trust your instincts.

A spirit guide appeared, and as she handed me a machete she said, "Are you ready? We're going to cut your ancestral cords."

For three nights I had visions of my mother's life, her pain and trauma from even before I was born, and then, like a projector in my mind, two bubbles appeared: To the left was my mother, the woman who had endured childhood trauma, who was lost and fighting to survive, who did the best she could with almost nothing and no one to guide her. On the right was the mother who owed me something, who was supposed to love me a certain way and didn't—she carried the weight of my expectations and disappointment. My heart softened, my tight grip and resentment released, I was able to see the difference between the woman and the mother, and I could accept that in this lifetime, she wasn't given a chance to embody the divine mother archetype. I saw that the woman hadn't been initiated into motherhood and was still carrying the emotional capacity of a small child. My heart opened and I dropped into acceptance of what I had missed out on as a little girl and deepened in compassion for why my mother couldn't give those things to me.

As I sat in with the medicine dozens of times over a span of six years, my ancestral wounds continued to unfold in ceremony. Darkness enveloped me as I faced the pain of feeling alone and the fear moving through my nervous system, the medicine forcing me to honor my grief. I stepped out of the anger and longing for a different story, and into the divine embrace of a higher universal energy. I felt father energy in all the good men who showed up for me in ceremony, to help me back to my mat or to sit with me in moments of fear. I found the mother within, and I found mother in the plants, the trees, the waters. As I began to heal, my mother wound began to shift too, without demand or expectation. I saw the power in my commitment to forge the path alone.

Some of us are here to break ancestral patterns of trauma, to end the cycle of passing down pain, abuse, addiction, and violence, and to begin to pass down love, humility, compassion, and truth. And if you are on this journey now, I see you. You are doing the most important work. Your helping ancestors are behind you.

EMBODYING THE ENERGY OF THE DIVINE MOTHER AND FATHER ARCHETYPE

Whether you believe that you choose your parents before being born into this world or you believe that it's all random, or something else, one vital pathway to finding a sense of empowerment and confidence is through individuation from your caregivers. This means stepping out of the role as the child with your parents and stepping into your adult self with an integrated capacity to care for yourself, provide self-nurturing, and trust your gut.

Divine mother and father energy is rooted in unconditional love, and it is all around you—it is in connecting to the energy of Spirit and to the natural world: the dirt, the wind and fire, the oceans, rivers and mountains. The four-legged, winged ones, the plants, and the trees—they all work together to nourish us, and one day we, too, are returned back to the earth. It is remembering that love is not something that exists outside of you; it is all that you are and everything you are made of. Whether you grew up with only one parent, or two mothers, or two fathers, or nonbinary parents, you have the ability to connect to this divine energy.

One warm summer day, my friend Anya sat next to me on my deck leading out to the expansive garden and treescape. We began talking about our journeys with the mother–father wound, and she shared her story with me.

When Anya was young, her dad passed away from an illness. Everything felt extremely chaotic and talking felt too hard. Often during breaks at school, she would quietly sneak away from her friends to go sit under an African tulip tree, a large tropical tree with bright red flowers. She laid under the tree's branches, between a few large roots, and felt held. "I was only thirteen, but it was a memorable moment of finding some peace," she told me. Anya described how nature had been her father's church, and how lying there under the falling tulips "felt like a way of being with him."

At home, she didn't feel she could express her sadness, anger, or how much she deeply missed him. Anya's mom was a very loving person, but she was so connected to her emotions that seeing Anya cry was very difficult for her. "My family was processing their own pain, and I don't think they had the capacity to hold mine too, so this tree became my place to quiet my thoughts and have some privacy with my pain," she said.

Anya spent much of her early adult life in anger and sadness that she had to be "the strong one," when what she needed most was space to express her grief. Through her own healing, Anya saw her mother's innocence and realized that her inability to be there for her wasn't rooted in maliciousness, but in love. And that even in her darkest moments, when she was in nature, she was never alone.

As young children, we love to play and *be* in nature. We instinctively know how to source divine energy in the elements. As adults, we often forget to come back to this innate source of healing. Whether it is an African tulip tree that holds us through an important moment or our toes digging into the earth, nature reminds us that we are still here and we will be okay; nature is where we break free from the mother–father wound and find peace. By releasing our parents from their roles, we accept that they are only human and we reclaim our healing instincts.

WAYS TO CULTIVATE DIVINE MOTHER AND FATHER ENERGY

Communicate with Your Inner Child

Imagine yourself from the position of a loving and nurturing parent. Listen to the needs and desires of "little you." Speak to your child self with love, kindness, and tenderness. Allow your child self to feel, play, and freely express vulnerability.

Be Discerning with Your Energy

Do you really want to do the thing? Be around that person? Have sex? Eat that food? Do you have to pee? It's the little moments of attunement with your body and responding to your needs that helps you tap into this energy.

Experience Divine Mother Energy in Nature

All the elements represent the divine mother—the oceans and rivers, the trees, grass, and flowers, wind and fire, earth and roots. Tapping into the universal energy of the divine mother through nature is a powerful way for you to reclaim your sensitivity and feel connected. Go for walks in nature and take time to really pause and listen to the sounds. Close your eyes and listen to the leaves rustle in the wind, the trees bending and swaying, the birds singing. Feel the rain falling, the sun kissing your skin, the snow on your cheeks. Dip your toes in the river, swim in the ocean, and feel the earth beneath your feet and your connection to the land that feeds you.

Call in Protective Energy

Protection is a signature characteristic of both the mother and the father. Though we most commonly associate protective qualities with the father, in nature, the last thing you want to cross is an animal mother with her babies. She is a fierce guardian and is not to be messed with. Protection is where the mother and father both embody fire. Tap into your own fierceness to set boundaries or protect your energy.

Set Boundaries with Your Inner Child

When your child self wants to act out, hold space for it lovingly while also stepping into the mature adult and not letting it take the reins of your experience.

Hold Yourself Accountable

Notice the urge to blame others. Take responsibility for your thoughts, feelings, and actions, and gently guide yourself toward intentional action.

Be the Authority of Your Life

You don't need to ask permission from other people to live the way you want to live. It's your life. You can be open to feedback while anchored to your own personal truth.

Prioritize Play and Laughter

Humans learn best when they are laughing! Embracing your inner joy and prioritizing play is one of the most vital things you can do for your well-being.

As you connect with divine mother and father energy, you may feel the call to express and resolve feelings toward your actual parents. If this is the case, I recommend you do the following letter ritual. Keep in mind that this process is for you to fully own and embrace your anger, resentment, or hurt so that you can release it.

You cannot bypass your way to acceptance, so allow yourself to be fully expressed in this ritual.

THE LETTER RITUAL

Write a letter to your parent. Tell them everything—all the hurt they caused, all the things you wished you could say to them, all the needs you wanted them to meet, all the ways they let you down, what you love about them, what you hate about them. Let it all out. This letter is for you, not for them. The deeper you go, the more you will get out of this process. *Note: Do not under any circumstances send this letter to your parent; this letter is for you alone.*

Heart-Opening Visualization: After writing your letter, sit with your eyes closed and connect to the energy of your parent. Imagine them as a small child; feel their innocence. Visualize a green and pink mist filling the space you're in, and see it emanating from your heart and transferring to theirs. Hold space for their innocence and yours. Allow warmth and compassion to naturally arise in you and, if it does, let it permeate your entire energy body.

Burning Ritual: You can place this letter on your altar, and when you feel ready (it could be on a new or full moon) you can burn it or put it in a bowl of water until it dissolves.

Closing Prayer: Place your hands on your heart and call in the energy of divine mother and father. Say out loud or in your head, "I release you from my expectations and the roles I've put you in. I am willing to see your innocence." As you sit in this quiet space, notice your energy and visualize yourself rooted to the earth. Invite in the divine embrace of Spirit to hold you and care for you; this loving connection is always available to you.

THINGS TO REMEMBER

- Acknowledging your mother–father wound is not about guilting or blaming your parent.

- You do not need to share your process with your parent. This work is for your own healing and liberation.

- Healing the mother–father wound is a slow, gradual process and requires that you feel your feelings and eventually find your way to acceptance and/or forgiveness.

- Very few of us grew up with parents who engaged in inner work; thus, most parents do not have the language to have hard conversations with you.

- Your parents are human beings with their own flaws, past traumas, and blocks. Their inability to show up for you in the way you needed is not a reflection of your worth.

- You can experience healing, transformation, and even an improved relationship with your parents by shifting your relationship to them in your own heart and mind.

- Mother and father energy can be found outside of your parents—in nature, and in yourself by learning how to self-nurture, take good care of your own heart, set boundaries, and honor your inner voice.

- Tapping into divine mother and father energy is a beautiful way to connect to universal love and nature; remember that you are not alone.

- You can do the letter ritual as many times as you need. Do not expect to do it once and feel complete.

Forgiveness is for you, not for them.
Your emotional experience is valid, but you may
never receive the external validation you crave.
Heal anyway.
You are the keeper of your story.
And it's never too late to write something new.

CHAPTER 7

FORGIVENESS AND ACCEPTANCE

DAKOTA HAD A VERY CLOSE RELATIONSHIP WITH HER father growing up. She loved to spend evenings after school telling him about her day and listening to him tell stories of his years working on a farm. Often, she would pull weeds alongside him in their herb garden instead of playing with the other kids in the neighborhood, just to spend more time with him.

Her parents didn't have a very happy marriage. They never fought, but they never seemed to touch each other or spend any time together—they didn't even sleep in the same room. When Dakota turned nine, her father packed a large tattered blue suitcase, filled his pickup truck with four cardboard boxes, and left. He called her for a few months to ask her about school, but eventually the phone calls slowed down until they lost their close connection altogether.

At the age of twenty-eight, Dakota was dating a man named Jacob, who often traveled for work and was gone for weeks at a time. Every night before he was meant to leave on another long business trip, she would lash out and frequently start big fights. She hated that their last nights together were often spent in conflict, and even though she was desperate to feel connected, her pride would cause her to wall up and ignore him until he left the next morning.

This pattern was destructive, and she wanted it to end. Over time, she realized that whenever Jacob was getting ready to leave, her inner child began to panic. The pain of her father leaving was being stirred up each time her partner was preparing to go away. In order to be present with her partner, Dakota had to make peace with her father and stop carrying the weight of her past resentment into the present day. Dakota began practicing inner child work, learned to self-soothe, and wrote letters to her father that she put on her altar and eventually burned. With time, she was able to forgive her father for leaving the way he did, and while she still felt tender when she thought of him, she no longer felt like she needed to leave her body. Instead, she was in acceptance of her story and, at times, even grateful for the opportunity to forge a beautiful connection with herself as she was healing.

Slowly, Dakota learned how to be vulnerable and find her center in her relationship with Jacob on the nights before he would leave. Rather than lashing out and pushing him away, she found that their nights together became intimate and connected. Finding forgiveness for her father ushered her into a place of safety and depth within herself. After some time, Dakota began to surrender and put her trust in life, knowing that, as an adult, she couldn't be abandoned anymore. And even if her partner did choose to take a different path, she knew she was going to be okay.

Forgiveness is a loaded word. It means something different to each of us, depending on our past experiences and the people we are with. It is about seeing the innocence underneath each of our layers of hurt. Forgiveness is a path of spiritual understanding and acceptance. It is not about perpetuating or allowing bad behavior or justifying someone's actions. Rather, it provides us with a deeper context of the human experience and offers us a way to set our hearts *free*—free from anger, bitterness, and resentment.

But healing these deep wounds takes time. It is a slow, nonlinear process that requires immense courage. It's normal to feel resistance to this part of the work, to be afraid to let go. The path to forgiveness can be scary because it means that we will inevitably have to feel all our hurt and sadness rather than shielding ourselves behind anger and blame.

While righteous anger is necessary and vital to our grief process, we can't stay in that energy forever. Without the final stages of softening, returning to our hearts, and embodying forgiveness, we remain locked in our story and the suffering never ends. Our vulnerability is the gateway to our power.

FORGIVENESS AS A PATHWAY TO FREEDOM

Have you ever laid in bed at night replaying a scenario in your mind of a small annoyance or hurtful thing someone did to you that day? Have you ever stood in the shower and played out the things you'd say to them if you had the chance?

We all need to be able to forgive people for minor infractions if we want to maintain healthy relationships. People hurt each other unintentionally and make mistakes all the time, and knowing when to forgive is vital. If forgiveness for the little things doesn't come easy for you, there's usually a story there. When we're quick to dismiss others or throw in the towel rather than attempting to repair, it's likely we're holding on to anger from the past that's preventing us from being in harmonious relationships. We may have blanket statements about how "all people" are a certain way, or see others through a cynical lens, always expecting things to turn out the same as they have before.

Feelings of betrayal or anger over the past can hijack our waking existence and hold us in a pattern of blame, resentment, and internal chaos. And while we may want the other person to take accountability for their actions before we let go, the hard truth is that holding a grudge comes at a high cost for us, not for them. **Unhealed and unresolved relationships with our parents, siblings, past partners, and past friends linger deep beneath the surface of our inner emotional world.**

Like Dakota with her father, when we hold on to our anger toward someone, they get to live rent free in our psyche, subconsciously affecting our outer lives. While these people may be blissfully unaware of their impact, we are the ones who suffer. Think of the process of forgiveness and acceptance like serving them an eviction notice. As long as we hold on to our resentment and replay past events in our mind, we're not free.

Sometimes in the process of moving on, we sequester our enemies and the memories that accompany them to the dark without ever really letting go. If any time you think of that person or experience and still feel negative emotion coursing through your body, this is a sign that it is a "charged" memory. What that "charge" is telling you is that they still hold a certain power over you. Without your knowing, this person may still be influencing your present reality. If we are unconsciously giving them energy, we may experience anxiety, exhaustion, and tension in our body.

Forgiveness isn't just about making peace with our past. Sometimes, forgiveness is and should be selfish. It's about taking back our power and no longer giving energy to someone who doesn't deserve a seat at our table. It's about clearing out anything that weighs us down and creating room in our consciousness for something or someone much more worthy.

When acknowledging the unresolved relationships in your history, be mindful that you can heal without needing anything from them. You don't need to reach out to an ex or your parents to get answers, explain yourself, or dredge up the past with people who you've been out of contact with for a long time. Only approach people from your past if there is a clear opening for this to happen and it feels truly aligned to do so. Remember, letting go isn't for them—it's for you. *Forgiveness is the road to internal freedom*, and it widens our capacity to open ourselves to love again, to trust ourselves and experience the depth and beauty life has to offer.

Journaling Session: Who Are You Carrying with You?

Find a quiet place and take ten to fifteen minutes to reflect. Write down a list of anyone you are still harboring anger, resentment, or unresolved feelings toward. Is there someone who hurt you that you may be carrying in your mind and heart? Is there a memory or someone who gives you a charged feeling, who still holds power over you? Hold on to this list, you will need it later in the chapter for the forgiveness ritual.

FINDING ACCEPTANCE FOR THE UNFORGIVABLE

As I matured in my perspective, it became easier for me to drop into forgiveness and compassion for my mom. I saw the trauma and abuse she was carrying in her own body from childhood, and instead of grieving what I didn't receive *from* her, I began to grieve *for* her. Grief for all the ways her own mother horribly failed her— far beyond any experience I ever had. What I came to realize is that while I had found forgiveness for my mother, I still carried so much rage and resentment toward my grandmother for all of the pain she had caused.

My grandmother was a very abusive and mentally unwell woman and the things she did were unspeakable. I couldn't make sense of the atrocities she committed against her own daughter. I couldn't access compassion or understanding; her abusive actions were far too great. To me, there was simply no way to make sense of what she had done.

Some things are unforgivable. It is right to feel angry when someone crosses boundaries. It is right to seek justice. And it is right to remove someone's energy from your life when they have caused you harm. You do not need to heal them with your love, or save them from their pain. That is their work to do, not yours. From this place, you can move toward acceptance.

Acceptance is important because without it, we're in resistance with ourselves. We may ruminate, wishing we could turn back the hands of time, writhing in remorse or thoughts of revenge, or seeing the world from a very bleak lens. When we can acknowledge what happened wasn't okay while also choosing to let in new possibilities, we're gifting ourselves the opportunity to live with our hearts open again.

Less about seeing another's innocence or understanding the root of their actions, acceptance is a willingness to acknowledge the past for what it is, with a knowing that we can't rewrite history or change the way things are. With acceptance, we can integrate our reality and make a conscious choice to see that good in the world still exists.

FORGIVENESS OR ACCEPTANCE DOESN'T MEAN

- You have to allow them back into your life
- They get a second (or third or fourth) chance
- What they did is okay, and they're no longer responsible
- You're minimizing the hurtful incident
- You're not entitled to your feelings about what happened

FORGIVENESS OR ACCEPTANCE DOES MEAN

- You accept what has happened cannot be changed
- You are valid in your feelings, and you are ready to feel something different
- You are ready to release yourself from replaying the event in your mind and nervous system over and over again
- You no longer want to give them power by holding on to anger and fear in your body

---

You Don't Have to Let Go
Before You're Ready

We're a culture that rushes to the finish line and puts a time stamp on grief.

But you don't have to move on and feel anything other than what's present for you now.

It's okay to hold on until you're ready to let go.

Make space for your anger, your rage, your sadness.

There are no goals to achieve or milestones to reach in the process of letting go.

The only requirement is that you feel to the depths of your being.

That you search in a way that your soul feels like searching,
that you seek in whatever way you need to seek.

And that you rest until your heart and body no longer
need the quiet winter that grief brings.

Don't listen to the spiritual idealists who tell you that your
"lower vibration" emotions are creating your reality, that you
only need to think positive, that you just have to "let go."

Hold on.

Hold on and let yourself have this experience.

Let go slowly, let go with intention, let go with care.

Letting go is a ceremony. It is a release of lost hopes, dreams, love, and life.

Bring reverence to your process. Let go slowly.

Peace will come.

EIGHT STAGES OF FORGIVENESS

Just like with grief, forgiveness comes in stages. In a way, it's hard to separate the process of grief from the process of forgiveness. We may encounter denial, anger, bargaining, depression, and acceptance before we finally feel at peace with our past.

Stage 1: Acknowledge What Happened
Are you in your head or in your body? When we've been hurt, we sometimes leave our body and shut down to avoid feeling the pain and anger. While you begin the process of moving toward

forgiveness, you need to make your way back to your body and acknowledge how you're feeling about what happened.

Stage 2: Feel Your Anger and Your Grief

We cannot rush the process of feeling our emotions around what occurred. Your anger and fire are just as acceptable and worthy of having a seat at the table as your love and forgiveness. We feel our way through the healing tunnel. No stone is left unturned. Wherever you are on your healing journey, know this:

> *Your anger is important.*
>
> *Your sadness is beautiful.*
>
> *Your voice matters.*
>
> *Your heart is innocent.*
>
> *It's safe to return to the truth of who you are.*

Stage 3: Get to the Hurt Underneath

In chapter 3 we talked about learning how to get to the feeling underneath a feeling. There are likely layers to your emotional reality that need to be felt and acknowledged before letting go happens. When you access states of defensiveness like anger or resentment, explore what might be underneath them until you reach a state of vulnerability.

Stage 4: Relate to Your Past

Explore how this situation may remind you of something that happened in your past, perhaps all the way back to your childhood. Is it harder to let go in this scenario, because the pangs of betrayal are rooted so deep in your history? Does this person represent something for you? If you need more help exploring this, you'll get to do this in the next chapter on understanding your projections.

Stage 5: Empathize with Your Own Hurt

When someone has hurt or wronged us, we long for someone to empathize with our experience. We want to be seen and understood. In the process of finding forgiveness, we must practice empathy toward ourselves and give attention to our inner child. Being in self-dialogue can look like placing your hands on your heart and asking your inner child, "If you had words for me, what would you say?" Let your heart speak and truly listen.

Stage 6: Validate Your Reality

It can be incredibly hard to move forward if you have felt invalidated in your experience. Working with a trusted guide or therapist who can offer empathy and validation during your process can be invaluable. However, if you don't have someone like that in your life, you may also be waiting to receive validation from someone who simply can't give it to you. Learning to self-validate is important so that you can trust yourself and heal on your own time line. Try some of these mantras to practice self-validating:

"I'm feeling _____ and that's okay."

"I can feel _____ and _____ at the same time."

"I have a right to feel how I feel in this situation."

"I did the best I could in this situation."

"My anger is welcome."

"My grief is welcome."

"My sadness is welcome."

"I deserve to feel peace."

Stage 7: Accept the New Reality

With any conflict, big change, or disruption in our lives comes a new reality. Whether we welcome or reject change, it's all we can count on for sure. When you've moved through the other stages, you'll find it's a lot easier to accept your new reality. If you notice you're in heavy resistance to accepting your present reality, it may mean you need to spend a bit more time on the other stages to give yourself space to process any lingering anger, resentment, or grief. Remember, there's no rush. You're not better or worse than anyone else if you take more time than your friend who was over it in a week.

Stage 8: Find Peace

When you've moved through all of the stages authentically, you will naturally come to find peace. As you move through these stages, you may find that you go back and forth between feeling complete and having surges of anger or grief return. This is normal, and you're not "regressing" in your process. New layers may come up for release for many more seasons, so make room for that to happen and stay curious as your process unfolds.

THE FORGIVENESS RITUAL

This ritual will support you in your forgiveness process. *(As with all letter rituals in this book, this is for you only. Do not send this letter to the person.)* Bring forward the list you created of people you may still be working on forgiving. Choose one person to focus on as you go through this ritual.

Write a Letter to the Person from the Past

- Say everything you want to say to them—don't hold back, even if it's rageful.

- Get as real as you possibly can. Remember, this is a therapeutic process for YOU, no one else.
- You may find that in your letter, you feel a mix of intense anger and intense sadness. Betrayal stings the most when we've opened our hearts to someone (a past lover, a parent, a friend) and that love was taken for granted.
- Write all the things you wanted from them and all the ways they let you down.

Try Expanding on These Sentences

You can use your own format for writing this letter. The following phrases can be really helpful to prompt you to dig deeper.

I'm angry at you because . . .

I hate you because . . .

I love you because . . .

Something I want from you is . . .

Something I'm afraid of is . . .

Something I want to say to you is . . .

The role I played in our relationship was . . .

Something I blame you for is . . .

Something I take responsibility for is . . .

I'm ready to accept . . .

I forgive myself for . . .

I'm ready to release you from . . .

As with the letter ritual provided in chapter 6, you can wait until you feel ready and burn the letter in a letting go ceremony. It's appropriate to place it on your altar until you feel an authentic sense of peace, acceptance, and readiness to let go.

THINGS TO REMEMBER

- Forgiveness is for you, not for them.

- Forgiveness can improve your physical well-being: better sleep, more energy, more openness in your body.

- Forgiveness returns you to the seat of your power and provides internal freedom.

- Forgiveness does not always mean reconciliation.

- Sometimes forgiveness looks more like acceptance so you can move forward.

- You cannot rush through the process of forgiveness; every stage along the way is valuable (grief, anger, acceptance, peace).

- You don't have to let go before you're ready; it's okay to take your time.

- Forgiveness is an organic process, and you don't need to force it.

- The end result of moving through the stages of forgiveness authentically is peace.

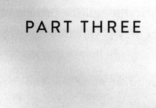

PART THREE

EXPLORE YOUR RELATIONSHIP PATTERNS

Our romantic partners are not our parents
or our children. To rise in love, we must
release them from our roles and labels and
make way for the mystery.

CHAPTER 8

UNDERSTANDING PROJECTIONS

LEARNING TO TRUST AND LET LOVE IN WHEN IT HASN'T been historically safe to do so is not easy. It's completely normal to be guarded when we've been hurt or betrayed in the past—without the ability to self-protect we wouldn't have evolved to where we are today. But that *same* instinct to self-protect can keep us separate from true intimacy and connection.

We keep love at a distance by *projecting* the people who hurt us in the past onto people trying to love us in the present. When our past hurt colors our current reality, we are bound by our projections. Freeing ourselves means learning to turn down the volume on the false alarms so that we can see things clearly. It also requires creating a sense of safety in our body so that we feel comfortable letting down our walls.

Love can stare us right in the face but if we're stuck in our projections, we won't be receptive to it. When we're projecting, extensions of love can feel suffocating, attempts to connect can feel like control, minor misunderstandings can feel devastating, and the overall climate of our relationships can feel unstable. On the other hand, we may have normalized relational dysfunction and find ourselves drawing in unsafe or harmful people, because that's all we've ever known. We may also find it difficult to navigate conflict or move through challenges in relationships without feeling the weight of the past pulling us back into chaotic emotional territory.

The way out of this is not to avoid relationships altogether, set rigid boundaries that prevent intimacy, or test a person until the straw breaks. The answer lies in our own healing. We don't escape pain by avoiding it; we heal by sitting in the fire and *being with* the intensity that arises as we relearn what it means to open our hearts and trust again.

Our identity is largely informed by our past. But this process is all about embracing the mystery of life by peeling back the layers of our known reality to make room for something more expansive. Let this process be a reorganizing of your conditioning so that *you*—not your past—are in charge of your future.

HOW PROJECTIONS INFLUENCE OUR RELATIONSHIPS

What exactly is a projection? It is the displacement of emotion and is often a hidden spot in our consciousness that can be tricky to identify. A *projection* is when we see a quality that exists in us or in someone from our past and we attribute it to something or someone outside of ourselves.

With projections, we see what we are wired to see. We may find ourselves easily triggered when a partner says or does something that reminds us of our history and so we superimpose red flags on them. In an instant, our loving partner disappears and all we see is every person who has ever hurt us. If we grew up with a parent who expressed their anger in dangerous ways, we might be hypervigilant when people close to us express anger. When we are projecting, even seeing a person who looks like our past partner may cause us to immediately dislike them, or feel wildly attracted to them. When we are in conflict with our partner, we may find that our complaints about them could easily be complaints we have had about our parents at some point in time. We may have someone who's committed and honest yet be unable to trust them because we've been hurt by someone else in the past.

Much of the chaos and heartache we have felt in our relationships is the result of unprocessed pain from our previous history.

KEEPING LOVE AT A DISTANCE

Harley's first girlfriend cheated on her when she was in high school. Even though her current girlfriend, Kim, was secure and trustworthy, Harley found herself flying into jealous fits anytime her partner even spoke to another woman. Kim was incredibly frustrated by this because she had never done anything to break trust in the relationship and it brought up an old familiar feeling of being misunderstood and wrongly accused of things she didn't do—a pattern that showed up in her family system. When Harley recognized she was projecting the relational rupture that happened in high school onto Kim, it opened up a door for them to talk about their family histories. As a result, they both felt more seen and they came to understand the projection for what it was, growing their capacity to respond rather than react in tough moments. Harley learned to ask for gentle reassurance when she needed it, and Kim was able to practice being present rather than getting defensive when Harley expressed her fears.

When we have not forgiven or made peace with old hurts, our partners can unconsciously represent a figure from our past— usually a caretaker, like our mother or father, but sometimes a sibling or teacher. We may find ourselves projecting a belief that the people in our lives now will be untrustworthy, unreliable, or emotionally unavailable, just as those in our past had been.

Projections are a defense mechanism, a way for our ego to protect us from our painful feelings. But projections also cut us off from love.

If the goal of the heart is togetherness and oneness, the goal of the ego is separateness. Think of the ego as your inner guard dog. If you've ever spent time with a rescue dog that has experienced trauma, you may have noticed that they are either extremely timid or extremely aggressive, barking and biting even when there is no real threat. It takes patience and time to teach them not to be constantly on edge or in a reactionary mode. And this is exactly what it's like when we ourselves have unhealed trauma looming over us in relationship. In a sense, working with your ego is like training your inner guard dog to be protective when it's really necessary, and to otherwise be warm, safe, and welcoming.

The ego is not bad; in fact, it is essential to our survival—it is what allows us to functionally engage with reality. It isn't until our ego begins to develop when we're young that we start to have an awareness of time and space and form an identity of our own. However, when we are wounded, the ego oversteps its function and takes on the role of ruthless defender, protector, and competitor. We don't want to eradicate or destroy it. Instead, we want to integrate it and give it space to exist, without assigning it an executive leadership position in our lives and relationships.

The more evidence we have from our past that vulnerability isn't safe, the more our ego will defend against it by unconsciously pushing people away and closing our hearts. When we notice ourselves wanting to self-protect, our work is to practice self-awareness and take a pause before reacting. While at times self-protection is vital, in intimate relationships where we're committed to love, our devotional practice is to go deeper by opening our hearts.

SEEING YOUR REALITY
THROUGH A SCRIPTED LENS

Yasuko's youngest son had a temper that reminded her of her mother's anger. This was very triggering for her, and she couldn't be as nurturing and understanding with him as she wanted to be. When he'd throw fits, she would revert to old dynamics that created more distance between them, criticizing him and shutting him out. During our sessions together, she did inner work around her mother wound. Over time, she was able to remain calm when her son was having an angry outburst and see him as a little boy who needed support rather than projecting her mother onto him. Yasuko reclaimed her role as the adult rather than the child in the relationship, and even though her son still had his moments, she was able to help soothe him instead of reacting like she had before.

When we're projecting, we force people into "roles" that fit the story we're running on. It could be the role of the Bully, the Angry Mother, the Absent Father, the Disapproving Teacher, or another figure from our history. In our relationships, we think we're fighting about one thing, but really we're fighting about something much older and deeper—the feeling of being dismissed or disrespected, unimportant or left out, just like when we were little.

As long as we are unconsciously seeking to close the loop, we will relive the experience again and again in hopes that, perhaps this time around, the ending will be different. But in order to have a different ending, we have to be in the present—to see people for who they are, rather than punishing them for the hurt others have caused us.

PROJECTIONS CAN LOOK LIKE

- Assuming your present partner will behave the way someone in your past did, such as a mother, father, or ex-partner

- Fear of being controlled in a relationship because a caregiver was controlling in the past

- Having a strong or negative reaction to something a person does because it touches on a painful past experience

- Unconsciously expecting a partner to rescue or take care of you (projecting a missing caregiver onto a partner)

- Being triggered by a friend or partner's sadness because a parent was emotionally unavailable due to their own depression

- Unconsciously punishing a present-day partner or relationship for something that happened in the past with another person

- Feeling triggered by someone who reminds you of a person who hurt you in the past

- Putting people on a pedestal; making yourself better or worse than others

IT'S NOT ABOUT THE NESPRESSO!

I'm going to share a funny story with you about a big fight Ben and I had on Christmas Day a few years back. We have had multiple miscommunications around gifts in our relationship, all with their own story to tell. We can look back now and laugh, but as you know, in the moment these things don't always seem so funny.

It was just a few months before Christmas, and I was sitting at the kitchen table when I said to Ben, "I think I want an espresso machine for Christmas!" I pulled up a beautiful Breville online (reasonably priced, I might add) and showed him a picture. "Like this!" I said.

Ben replied, "What about a Nespresso?" and I said, "Please don't ever get me a Nespresso, I hate those things!"

Months went by and I really didn't think about it again. Then, on Christmas Day while we were waiting for his parents to arrive, I said to him, "Let's open gifts before they get here." I just had a gut feeling that I didn't want an audience. He insisted we wait and open them together, and I reluctantly agreed.

My in-laws came over, and we had dinner and then opened some presents. Ben wrote me the most beautiful card, and as I read it, my heart filled with so much love. If he had given me nothing but that card, I would have been 100 percent fulfilled. Next, he put a big box on the table. I tore off the wrapping paper and—you guessed it—it was a damn Nespresso box! "He must be pranking me," I thought quietly to myself. "There's no way he'd actually get me the very thing I told him I didn't want." But as he looked at me bright-eyed with a big smile on his face, and I realized that, indeed, there was a Nespresso in the box, I became deflated and tried to act surprised in front of my audience.

Just as I thought the gift-giving portion of our night had ended, he stood up and I looked behind me to see a big blanket on the floor covering up more gifts. He ripped the blanket off and you know what was underneath? Boxes and boxes of dozens of Nespresso pods . . . *Dozens, I tell you!* I didn't know what to say, so I just walked out of the room and Ben and his dad went to put the machine together.

Later that night we went on a walk, and we had it out . . . or more accurately, I had it out. I was so upset, I was crying and absolutely livid about this gift. While I knew his heart was in the right place, in that moment I was distracted by my own internal story.

So, why am I telling you this? Because, it was never about the Nespresso machine. Like I said, he could have just given me a card and I would have been happy! It wasn't about the gift; it was about that old, aching familiar feeling of being invisible, of not feeling heard.

In gifting me something that I specifically told him I didn't want, I felt unseen, and this triggered the little girl in me that was never heard growing up. Bouncing around from foster home to foster home as a kid, being labeled as "bad" by my teachers because I was in the system, and not being allowed to play with certain friends because their parents thought I would be a negative influence all made an imprint on me. Even now, having done a lot of healing work, I am still sensitive to feeling misunderstood, unseen, and not heard.

If I didn't have the history I do, I might have just laughed at him and said, "Thanks, babe!" and told him I didn't really like the gift. But it tapped into something very old that was clearly still alive within me. It brought up so much emotion that it caused me to lose sight of reality and believe there was a big problem in our relationship when the truth is, Ben loves me. Sometimes he forgets things just like the rest of us, and that is not a reflection of his care for me or his willingness to keep growing in love.

Because my script was that the people closest to me don't see me, the Nespresso machine served as evidence and fit perfectly into my story. "You never listen" and "you always" may have been said a few times during that fight. It's not that I wasn't valid in feeling upset that Ben didn't listen to me, but when we're projecting, the emotional charge that accompanies a conflict is often inflated, creating more disconnection and clouding our ability to speak our true feelings. If we want to navigate our conflicts with grace and understanding, we have to bring awareness to our history and that of the people we love, so we can relate to one another with clarity of heart.

HOW TO HEAL YOUR PROJECTIONS

When we're in a projection, our nervous system gets activated and our ego tightens its grip. We may become more defensive, stubborn, unavailable, dismissive, avoidant, anxious, or even mean. No matter what a person does or says, if we're seeing through a past lens, it's not going to make a difference. This means we can easily turn someone into an enemy in our mind and push them away even if what we really want is for them to come closer.

The first step to healing your projections is to grow your capacity to be with your own discomfort when it arises. Most of the time, a projection is hard to catch in the moment because the trigger feels so real that we justify our reactions. When the intensity of the emotion is too much, we try to offload it or make it someone else's problem. By sitting with our body's sensations and naming them instead of projecting them through accusatory language, criticism, and defensiveness, we can transform a painful memory into a healing moment. One where we can release the old story and create the kind of connection and intimacy we truly want.

A brief moment of pause can give us the self-awareness that we need to recognize when we are projecting and come back to center. In doing this, we are building a bridge between our past self and our present self so that we can tell our body and brain that we are safe. The person in front of you today is not your mother, father, teacher, or caregiver. They likely reflect similar behaviors and qualities to someone from your past, but they are an entirely different person with their own unique history, traumas, and stories.

The more we can see others for who they really are, the more clarity we will have in choosing friends and partners wisely.

Once while Ben and I were in conflict, I was giving him a lecture about all the ways he didn't show up for me, when I suddenly froze and realized everything I was saying to him could have easily been said to my mother. When I checked into reality, what I was saying about Ben wasn't meant for him at all. My pride wouldn't let me own it right then and there, but a few hours later, I had to take accountability for hurling my wounds at him unfairly. And sometimes, that's the best we can do. What's important is that we make the effort to consistently own our emotional reality.

Healing your patterns doesn't mean you'll never find yourself in a similar situation again (you most likely will, as old patterns die hard). But what it does mean is that you'll have a chance to respond more gracefully and act from your truth rather than your wounding.

HOW TO TELL WHEN WE'RE PROJECTING

- We feel out of control in our reactions.
- Our anger seems uncalibrated to the situation.
- We become unwilling to consider alternative realities.
- We are convinced we know the other person's intentions.
- We think we know exactly how things will turn out.

NAVIGATING EMOTIONALLY CHARGED MOMENTS

The more emotionally charged you feel about a situation, the greater the chances are that the emotional intensity is connected to more than whatever you're fighting about on the surface. Your feelings are valid, and your emotional experience matters, yet it's important not to focus entirely on the first reaction that comes to you.

If you're pushing love away in a moment when you really want connection, you may be self-sabotaging. This is your inner child crying out to you, asking to be heard. It might seem easier to ignore our role in our patterns and place all the responsibility on others, but in the end, this only leads to more disappointment because what most of us truly want is to be seen and valued.

Underneath our projections and defensiveness is always a vulnerability. Your mission is to begin making friends with your vulnerability and tending to it daily, especially in highly charged moments. Tending to your vulnerability can look like speaking loving words to yourself, letting loved ones see you when you don't have it all together, or having a good, cleansing cry. When we drop our defenses and make room for our own humanity, we can develop an honest inner dialogue with ourselves.

Increasing Awareness in Moments of Emotional Intensity

The next time you find yourself in conflict, or on the defense, take a break from the situation at hand. You can't solve problems when you're triggered. Instead, step back and walk yourself through this self-centering exercise to get at the heart of the issue:

1. Take a few deep breaths. Put your hands on your heart and belly.

2. Connect to your body and name your emotions and sensations. This will help bring you back to the present moment.

3. Now tune in, and ask yourself:

   - *What am I feeling?*
   - *What does this bring up for me?*
   - *Who or what does this person remind me of?*
   - *What feelings am I trying to push away right now?*
   - *What do I really need that I'm afraid to ask for or don't believe I can have?*
   - *What am I afraid to say? What am I afraid to feel?*

4. Notice the sensations in your body, such as tingling, tightness, heat, contraction, or fluttering.

5. As you notice the sensations, simply breathe and be with them for a moment.

6. Notice a place in your body that feels calm, relaxed, and open.

7. Breathe into that calm, relaxed, and open place and be with that experience.

Here's an example of a realization someone might have after slowing down and reflecting on the root of their intense emotions and defensiveness: *Right now, I'm blaming and attacking, but underneath the blaming and attacking is deep sadness and anger. What I really need right now is to know that I am loved, and that my partner is not going anywhere. I'm afraid of being abandoned. This situation reminds me of when I was little and I was ignored whenever I expressed big emotions.*

The more layers you go into feeling what's under the feeling, the closer you get to the core of the issue. It is not enough to try and think your way out of a trigger or deeply activating moment. Your inner guard dog needs to know that it's safe before it leaves the front lines, and for this to happen, your nervous system needs to get on board.

THE WISDOM OF OUR PROJECTIONS

We tend to oversimplify projection to mean that whatever we see in our relationships must not be valid because it's a projection. But you can be projecting *and* be in a dynamic that isn't healthy. As you move into the following chapters, we'll explore the difference between a red flag and a false alarm to help you determine when to set a boundary and when to lean in.

Healing our projections gives us the power to see our relationships for what they are. It allows us to recognize when we are unconsciously trying to win love from someone because they remind us of a parent, and instead make the choice to walk away. Sometimes we're being shown where we consistently self-abandon or allow others to cross our boundaries, or the areas where we bend or change ourselves to fit into someone else's life, rather than being who we truly are. Sometimes what projections are really showing us is where we are ready to grow.

We all project in our relationships; it's human nature and never goes away completely.

The best way to shift out of the habit of projecting heavily in your relationships is to learn how to identify when you are caught in the projection and move outside of it. We do this by getting honest with ourselves and being willing to own when we're stuck in a story.

Healing our projections allows us to step out of the drama and into the world where we can be of service. At some point in our healing, we have to go beyond ourselves and begin to give back. This journey is a preparation for you to come home to yourself so that you can share your energy with the world in a way that is impactful, heart-centered, and in alignment with your soul's purpose.

THINGS TO REMEMBER

- A projection is when you're experiencing a wound or betrayal from the past as if it's happening in the present moment.

- When you're caught in a projection, you may experience an intense emotional charge toward someone and have a hard time seeing things from their perspective or navigating conflict in a healthy way.

- When emotions are high, it's not the time to get to the bottom of things. Focus on self-soothing and processing your experience, and then come back to the issue.

- Being aware of your projections is one of the key steps in breaking unhealthy cycles in your relationships.

- We all project and there's nothing to be ashamed of, but how we handle those projections when they come up will shift as more healing occurs.

Some of us are here to be the changemakers
in our family system. We're here to end
generational trauma and start passing down
love instead of pain.

CHAPTER 9

TRANSFORM YOUR RELATIONSHIP PATTERNS

PEOPLE OFTEN COME TO THIS WORK EXPECTING TO completely eliminate something—an old way of being, a behavior, or a belief. We hope to break our patterns and wash our hands of them for good. And we think that if we could just stop this one thing, we will feel loved and whole. *If I could just stop dating the "unavailable" ones. If I could just stop being so critical of others. If I could just stop being so needy.* But we do not transform our patterns by eradicating them; in fact, when we seek to eradicate them, we give them even more energy.

Everything is energy. We either fuel or starve our patterns depending on how we choose to direct our energy. If we really want to shift a pattern, we must learn to channel our energy mindfully. Our emotions and our patterns operate on an energetic frequency. When our energy isn't contained, we can mismanage it by giving it away to whatever drama presents itself in our lives—we may put energy into seeking revenge, holding on to resentment, and behaving reactively. We might indulge in senseless arguments or create friction in our relationships just to feel something. If we look at energy like a ladder, the very bottom of the ladder is our lowest form of expression: unconsciousness, hatred, and destruction; at the top of the ladder, we have consciousness, love, and expansion. As we make our evolution up the ladder, we are transforming our energy to a higher octave by consciously directing it rather than letting it spill out of us erratically.

Our patterns naturally transform as we learn how to harness our energy responsibly. Everything has two sides: love and hate, light and dark, positive and negative, internal and external. They are one and the same, though their impact is vastly different depending on the frequency of expression. This is what we're going to work on in this chapter. You'll learn how to see every pattern and response in your life as energy and you'll develop the consciousness to properly direct your energy toward behaviors, responses, and choices that enhance your life and invite in more harmony. In each moment you have a choice: *Do you want to feed this pattern with your energy? Or do you want to stop giving it energy and direct all that power toward something else?* To transform, we need to stop feeding the patterns we are ready to transcend.

WHAT'S A RELATIONSHIP PATTERN?

Kenya always seemed to attract the unavailable, "rough around the edges" type. During a session together, after months of feeling exhausted with dead-end dates, she shared with me her excitement when she met Jacq. Their beautiful future started to take shape in her mind as Jacq showered her with love, gifts, and affection. They went on romantic dates and the sexual chemistry was off the charts!

But then out of nowhere, Jacq began to pull away. For days, Kenya wouldn't hear from them. She was devastated and filled with anxiety, asking herself what she did wrong. They'd come back days or even weeks later filled with excuses, telling her how much they had missed her.

She'd let them back in thinking, *If I just make everything easy for them, they won't leave again.* So, she cooked, lent them money, showered them in affection, and dropped everything when they called. She never voiced her opinions or said no to an invite in hopes that they would stay this time. After going back and forth like this for months, Jacq eventually ghosted her completely. Unfortunately, this wasn't the first time Kenya had a relationship end like this. And it wasn't until she realized her *pattern of self-abandonment* that she began shifting her energy.

When she noticed anxiety in her body, instead of reacting to it the way she used to by giving herself away, she poured energy back toward her self-care. She'd prepare herself a meal, go on a walk, or take care of something in her practical life that would add to her sense of security and inner peace. She also made an effort to move through her resistance when it came to saying no and became more discerning about whom she shared her time with. Through this shift, Kenya was able to interrupt the cycle and attract an available partner where she was free to be herself—boundaries and all.

Even though we may end up with different people, we can find ourselves in the same situation with the same merry-go-round of conflicts, disappointments, and challenges. As much as we may try, we cannot outrun our relationship patterns. Instead, our patterns come with us wherever we go, presenting themselves once again in each new partner we bond with. We may be enamored at first by the initial rush of a new connection, but sooner or later, real life sets in and we're right back where we started. Once again, we find ourselves in the same old power struggle, experiencing hauntingly similar frustrations as we have in our past relationships.

These patterns are our relational growth edges and the work our soul has come here to do in this lifetime. But once you realize a pattern—"I close myself to love," "I'm afraid to be in my power with someone I love," "I lose myself in the other," or whatever it may be—the evolution of the pattern has begun. Becoming aware of your habits gives you an opportunity to be more conscious about which channel you choose to operate from.

COMMON RELATIONSHIP PATTERNS WE MAY FIND OURSELVES IN

- Engaging in the anxious-avoidant dance
- Running at the first sign of conflict
- Instigating conflict and creating chaos any time things start to feel secure
- Often being left for another person
- Repetitive cheating or being cheated on
- Chasing unavailable/emotionally unsafe people
- Losing touch with self when in a relationship
- Going from dangerous to overly safe partners but never having both passion and emotional intimacy
- Fearing deep intimacy (eye contact, closeness)
- Holding back true expression
- Becoming a chameleon ("I'll be whoever you want me to be.")

As we begin healing our relationship patterns, what we are really doing is "unlearning" the ways we've come to defend our hearts throughout our lifetime. We are learning to move into a secure place within ourselves by rebuilding a healthy connection to our body, emotions, and inner world. The hallmarks of being secure are being able to maintain long-term relationships, receive support when needed, trust others, and enjoy a high level of self-esteem.

In a sense, it feels safer to stay in the pattern we're in (even if it's painful), rather than letting go of our conditioning and sitting in the uncertainty of it all. Unlearning isn't easy. In fact, it's disorienting, and, often, disappointing. It can be disturbing to see the ways in which we have perpetuated our own chaos in relationships. But the power to heal lies in recognizing that even when we have made mistakes, we are worthy of experiencing healthy love. One of the best ways to practice being secure in any relationship is through friendships. These are containers where we can bring our vulnerable selves to the table, be curious and open, and practice setting boundaries. As you begin to embody this work, remember that you can bring these principles into every relationship in your life.

WHAT IS YOUR RELATIONSHIP SIGNATURE?

Each of us carries a unique *relationship signature* that follows us throughout our lives. Shaped by our earliest attachments, it is the blueprint for how we relate to others on a romantic level and our tendencies when we begin to get close to someone. Some of us tend to move away from connection while others are more likely to move toward it, sometimes to the point where we lose ourselves in the process.

We get stuck in old patterns when we continue to operate from the belief that the issue lies solely with our partner or the relationship itself without recognizing that we are the common denominator in all our experiences. We are being invited to shine a light inward and ask ourselves the hard questions. **The first and most important question is, *What is this pattern trying to teach me?***

If we are mindful and attentive, we can begin to see the ways in which our partners, and the relationships we choose, are revealing the parts of us that want to emerge, be seen, and heal. They are where our unconscious fears and deepest wounds are activated.

Sometimes the pattern is showing us that we need to voice our needs more and set firmer boundaries. Sometimes it is showing us our codependent or people-pleasing tendencies. Or our fear of intimacy, of being hurt and abandoned, or the existential dread of being broken. For some of us, our lesson is to learn how to lean into the challenges and stop running from intimacy. For others, our lesson is to say, "Enough is enough" and walk away. We're all here to learn, and the lessons that arise are unique to our personal life path.

Understanding your relationship signature will help you decode your attachment patterns and what your personal lessons are in your relationships. While there are three main archetypes—ocean, mountain, and wind—your relationship signature is not a box to put you in or an identity to attach to. As human beings, we are incredibly dynamic, and attachment is very nuanced. You may see aspects of yourself in all of the archetypes, and that's normal. Most commonly, you will find that you relate to one archetype more than the others.

Read through the signature descriptions and see which one resonates most (if you would like to take the quiz online, you can also go to BTOQuiz.com).

OCEAN TYPE

Empowered Expression: Caring and nurturing, expressive, attentive, intuitive, sensitive, loves fully, deep thinker, dreamer.

Greatest Challenge: You may find yourself anxious and ungrounded in relationships, or obsessive and in need of constant reassurance. You may have a tendency to self-abandon and ditch friends or personal interests for a partner. Seeking a sense of control, you can be hyper-critical of people you're in relationship with and hold impossibly high expectations of others.

Your Practice: To learn how to stay true to yourself in a relationship, show up fully, and ask for what you want even during conflict. Your practice is also to learn how to self-soothe so you don't feel desperate, anxious, or afraid when conflict arises or when you're dating.

MOUNTAIN TYPE 〈〉〈

Empowered Expression: Stable, sincere, trustworthy, loyal, committed, reliable, caring, wise, patient, consistent with friendships and hobbies even when romantically partnered.

Greatest Challenge: Mountain types have a tendency to over-give, become the caretaker, be "the strong one," and put everyone else's issues above yours. Attracting avoidant or needy partners, you can often feel lonely, like few people get your depths. You can also take on the role of teacher or coach in your relationships and find the dynamic draining over time.

Your Practice: To step out of the caretaker role and let yourself be supported sometimes. Ask for help, even if you know you can do it on your own. Give people a chance to figure things out for themselves and remember that it's not up to you to save or fix anyone. Know when to cut the cord and end a relationship, and when it's time to lean in and do the work. Remember, it takes two willing people, and you can't save everyone.

WIND TYPE 〜〜

Empowered Expression: Self-sufficient, like living life on your own terms, freedom oriented, thrive with alone time, find solitude reenergizing, resourceful and good at problem-solving, natural leadership abilities.

Greatest Challenge: Can sometimes be dismissive or have an impact on others without realizing it. You tend to be unpredictable and intense and struggle to show emotion or vulnerability, avoiding deeper states of intimacy or becoming intensely turned off by "clingy" behavior. You may also experience extreme loneliness and feel like people don't get you or can't meet you where you are.

Your Practice: To learn how to be in a relationship with another while still maintaining a feeling of being free. Rather than avoiding conflict, wind types are being invited to learn how to sit with uncomfortable feelings for long enough to come back into harmony with friends or lovers. Your practice is to share your feelings and learn how to express yourself fully rather than holding back or hiding.

THE FALSE BELIEFS THAT FUEL OUR PATTERNS

If self-awareness, safety, and devotion are the fuel for conscious relationships, then false beliefs are the fuel for our negative patterns. Our society is so littered with false beliefs about relationships that we may not even realize we've taken on those beliefs and embedded them in our own framework for how we view love.

The belief that we can either have hot chemistry or safe love and not both, that conflict isn't normal, that the right relationship will make our problems go away, that our partners will save us from our past, that marriage and commitment mean no sex, or that we have to put people through the wringer before we trust them are all classic false beliefs that limit us from having what we want. But we don't have to subscribe to these old, played-out narratives that reinforce a culture of disconnection and relationship drama. With intention and willingness, we can cocreate passionate, trustworthy, and spiritually alive partnerships.

Dysfunctional relationship patterns are sustained on our internalized fears and limiting beliefs. What follows are some of the fears that may be buried in our psyche that perpetuate our relationship struggles. Consider your own beliefs. Think about how you see yourself in relationships. Is there a belief that continues to resurface in your relationships?

- I'm not enough.
- I'm too much.
- Everyone leaves me.
- My emotions are unlovable.
- I need to be rescued.
- I don't deserve to be happy.
- I have to work hard to earn love.
- I have to be the rescuer in my relationships.
- I'll always be broken.
- I can't let anyone get too close.
- No one understands me.

Acknowledging the false beliefs we carry gives us the self-awareness to drastically shift how we relate to others. When we claim ourselves as whole and worthy, we convey through our bodies and our energy that we are ready to show up for life. Leaving our limitations at the door, we can open ourselves to being known in love.

THE UNCONSCIOUS CONTRACTS
WE MAKE WITH OURSELVES

Virginia Satir was an influential psychotherapist who made a grand contribution to the field of family therapy. In the 1950s her work was anything but mainstream—she discovered that all families had unconscious contracts or unspoken agreements that everyone in the family was expected to follow. Unconscious contracts were usually the parents' way of feeling in control and keeping things familiar, even if they were dysfunctional, disconnected, or limiting to the rest of the family.

We all have unspoken agreements in our relationships, but the more we examine our values and our parental conditioning, the more we are able to release ourselves from "rules" that no longer serve a useful purpose or that cut us off from our authentic self.

How Unconscious Contracts Can Play Out

Sonja was a hardworking mother of two children. Her parents emigrated from Taiwan before she was born, and she always felt like she had a foot in two worlds. In her household, it wasn't okay to rest: "You must work hard and take what you can get" was the mantra of her parents, who had to work tirelessly to survive in a new country. Sonja worked morning to night and filled every gap in her schedule with something to do. She wanted to spend more time with her boys, but her schedule was so full and she began to feel like she was missing out on their best years together.

As she got older, she started to realize that she couldn't stop doing—she didn't know how to truly relax. In fact, she wasn't sure whether she had ever really taken a true break in her life. In unwinding that pattern, Sonja realized that she had been working herself to the bone to keep an unconscious contract with her parents—which was ironic, because even her parents were now telling her to rest more! She began to slowly find little spaces in her schedule to practice doing nothing. She couldn't believe how much pressure she had put on herself for all those years. Sonja found freedom in breaking the old agreement and entering a new one that she consciously created to spend more time playing and relaxing with her children.

COMMON UNCONSCIOUS CONTRACTS
AND FALSE BELIEFS

- Don't show your weaknesses to others (emotions equal weakness).
- Anger is unacceptable/dangerous (you aren't allowed to get angry).
- Don't speak up or share your opinion (don't take up space).
- Always be striving, achieving, and working (it's not okay to rest).
- Money is bad; it's not okay to be abundant (money makes you selfish).
- We keep our family matters private (it's not okay to be vulnerable or ask for help).
- Having boundaries is selfish (we're enmeshed).
- It's my job to keep the peace, no matter the cost (I'm responsible for everyone).
- My parent needs me for emotional support (it's my job to be the caretaker/I can't receive).

It's important to remember that the reason we agree to these unconscious contracts in the first place is so that we can feel a sense of security and belonging within our family system. Stepping outside of our assigned role can feel dangerous. It taps into our fear of being ostracized. All humans have a deep need for belonging, so most of us play along, even if it means we abandon ourselves in the process. In the absence of these old contracts is our chance to think about what kinds of habits and rituals we'd like to pass down to the generation below us—something wise to think about, whether we choose to be parents or not.

WHY WE CHASE
EMOTIONALLY UNAVAILABLE PEOPLE

If it's your pattern to find yourself attracted to people with emotionally unavailable or avoidant tendencies, your inner work is to look at the ways you are abandoning or running from *yourself*. Sometimes other people can act as a distraction from feeling what's inside. If we're too busy trying to earn the validation and love of another, we don't really have time to slow down and be with the parts of ourselves that we don't feel are worthy or lovable.

What if all the energy you spent on chasing, competing, and trying to force something to happen was redirected toward self-reflection? Sometimes we're caught in a loop with emotionally unavailable people because we are, on some level, afraid of being seen fully and completely. *Chasing unavailable love is the same as avoiding available love.*

To break this pattern, we have to be willing to see how our deep-seated fears and wounds from the past can keep an old story alive, long past its expiration date. If you find yourself chasing a relationship or partner, dive deep. What feeling are you trying to attain? Is it love? Acceptance? Safety? Validation? Be honest with yourself. There's nothing to feel ashamed of. Whatever it is, know that whoever you're pursuing isn't the one who can give you these things. What are the parts you are trying to hide? Commune with them. What are your deepest desires? Declare them. What do you want to feel? Cultivate that. Your work is to practice self-validating and remaining true to yourself, connected to your body and to your core values.

CHOOSE YOUR CHANNEL

For those of us who grew up in chaotic environments where love was deeply conditional, or where emotional nurturance and care were unavailable, we might be turned on by the chase. We might feel a rush of excitement when there's turbulence or drama, and that's not because we're messed up or want the worst for ourselves—it's our emotional programming. It's what we know.

I personally understand this pattern all too well. In my younger years I was addicted to the honeymoon phase, to the rush of chemicals that followed new and difficult romance. I was always seeking externally, and I was always deeply unhappy the moment things began to feel calm in my relationships. But because I had no baseline for healthy love, and I didn't understand that relationships weren't always full of sudden change and intense highs and lows, I just figured something was wrong when the intensity wore off.

As a child, I went from foster home to foster home (attending eight elementary schools during seven grades!). My "normal" was chaos. My nervous system was wired for constant upheaval and change. It wasn't until I dove deep into my own healing work that I began to notice the pattern. Whenever I'd start to feel antsy, I would pick apart my relationship. The more routine and steady the relationship got, the more I saw it as passionless and dull. So, I'd burn my life to the ground and start all over again.

As I began to identify this in myself, I had an opportunity to learn how to work with the pattern rather than try to eradicate it. **Instead of turning my life upside down, I found ways to transmute the energetic attraction to chaos by nurturing my relationship with adventure and creativity.**

When I'd start to feel that stirring within me, I'd speak it out loud to myself and remind my body that I deserve to have a calm and secure existence. Then, I'd find a way to give my inner child what she craved in a healthy way. I'd plan a camping trip. Redecorate a room in the house. Start a project. I found ways to channel that energy into something productive that helped me heal my life rather than implode it.

As I did this more and more, my relationship to chaos transformed to the point where my nervous system rewired to not just enjoy calm and security, but to crave it. If I had chosen to ignore this pattern because I was ashamed or afraid of it, I may likely still be under its control today. I didn't heal by getting rid of it; I healed by acknowledging it was a part of me, and then deciding how I would work with the energy of the pattern.

Some of the most destructive figures in the world and in our media are also the most creative people—they simply mismanage their energy. If you look at most villains in movies, they are often highly intelligent and very powerful. The problem is, they've given their energy over to a vacuum of consumption, revenge, and destruction. But if those same characters chose to channel their energy differently, they could have changed the world for the better. All of us have this capacity—we get to choose our channel. Will we siphon our energy away to the never-ending drama that pulls for our attention, or will we see the distraction for what it is and bring mindfulness to where we put our energy?

Healing our relationship patterns doesn't mean the pattern will completely vanish. But what does change is the intensity and the ability to work through them without burning the house down. We rewrite our story by transforming the *behaviors* that accompany our patterns, learning how to respond to our fears, anxieties, and relationship conflicts with grace, rather than reacting from our wound.

UNCOVER YOUR RELATIONSHIP PATTERNS

Now, we are going to go step by step through an exercise intended to support you in uncovering the theme of your own relationship patterns. This exercise will help you develop self-awareness and draw attention to the ways in which you can set healthy boundaries and align with your truth.

Relationship patterns are common threads that weave together from one relationship to the next. Everyone has a pattern in their relationships, and in their life at large. This is not always a problem, but when the pattern results in you or a partner feeling underappreciated, abandoned, not enough, or too much, then it's worth looking at.

Remember, in learning how to witness the pattern as it arises and embrace it, you reduce its power. If you find yourself falling into self-judgment during this exercise, redirect yourself to self-compassion. **The self-judgment and rejection of the pattern are the glue that ensure you stay there.** Instead, when the pattern shows up, see if you can relate to it with understanding and perhaps even bring humor into the observation.

If you have a friend who's going through this book with you or if you're in a book club for *Becoming the One*, you can ask your interview partner to offer you reflections and ask you more questions to help you gain deeper insight into your answers.

STEP 1: EXPLORE YOUR EARLY EXPOSURE TO RELATIONSHIPS, SEX, AND LOVE

Here you will answer questions about your parental relationship. Exploring this relationship will give you insight into how you view and experience other relationships.

Questions to Ask Yourself

- What was your parents' relationship like? Were they together, married, divorced?

- How did they get along? Was there fighting, passive-aggressive behavior, loving and open communication, smothering, jealousy, cheating, honesty, secrecy?

- How did your father behave around your mother?

- How did your mother behave around your father?

- Did you ever see your parents engage in lovemaking, physical affection, or words of affirmation?

- What were your earliest thoughts, ideas, or beliefs about marriage or what a relationship was supposed to be like?

- What were your earliest thoughts, ideas, or beliefs about sex?

- Did your parents talk to you about sex? What did they tell you?

- Did your parents talk to you about love, connection, and relationships? What did they tell you?

- How did you feel around boys or men when you were growing up? For example, did you feel safe, unsafe, scared, excited, uncomfortable, at ease, or safer than with women?

- How did you feel around girls or women when you were growing up? For example, did you feel safe, unsafe, scared, excited, uncomfortable, at ease, or safer than with men?

STEP 2: EXPLORE YOUR RELATIONSHIP HISTORY

Start at your first significant romantic relationship and work your way up to your last relationship, or the one you're presently in.

Questions to Ask Yourself

- How did the relationship start?
- How long was the relationship?
- What feelings did you experience most frequently within the relationship?
- What were your conflicts usually about?
- What was the emotional landscape of your partner? Were they loving, avoidant, anxious, aggressive, jealous, attentive?
- How did the relationship end?

STEP 3: UNCOVER YOUR PERSONAL RELATIONSHIP PATTERN

Now you can go over everything you've discovered and see whether you notice any themes. You may notice similarities in things like physicality, profession, or personality or you may struggle to find any similarities at all. Where you will uncover the most information about yourself is in the emotional theme—the common emotional experience of each relationship.

Questions to Ask Yourself

- Did you go back and forth between two types of partners, such as the "safe and boring" type and the "dangerous and sexy" type?

- Did you experience some form of betrayal in each relationship, such as lying or cheating?

- Did you commonly feel unseen, unheard, frustrated, unimportant, or some other emotional experience?

- Do you attract avoidant or anxious types primarily?

- Are you more drawn to people who are not available either emotionally or because they are already with a partner?

STEP 4: WORK WITH YOUR ENERGY

Your practice is not to reject the pattern whenever it shows up, but to play with it more artfully. Life loves to test us, and there are endless opportunities to practice shifting our energy—when someone cuts us off when we're driving, when a person we're close with disappoints us, when we're having an off day. Moment by moment, we are choosing our responses. As you become aware of your energetic impact, you become a practitioner mindfully harnessing your energy and directing it toward authenticity and truth.

THINGS TO REMEMBER

- Everything is energy. Your patterns transform when you learn to harness your energy in a more empowering direction.

- You don't need to "fix" or get rid of your relationship patterns.

- Integrating your patterns means you accept them and can respond with maturity rather than letting your wounded inner child run the show.

- Relationship patterns are a reflection of your first family conditioning, belief systems, and unconscious contracts.

- Your relationship patterns are your work to undertake in this lifetime. They may never fully go away, but how they show up will shift and soften as you heal and integrate.

- When you step into your most empowered self and embody maturity in your relationships, the same patterns that once rocked your world will now hold beautiful opportunities for vulnerability and connection.

Don't punish yourself for the way you acted out
your pain when you were in survival mode.

Honor your walls for the protection they gave you.

Trust your heart.
Your innocence has always been there.

Let a new story birth itself from all you have
learned and overcome to be here now.

CHAPTER 10

COMPASSIONATE SELF-AWARENESS

AS CHILDREN, MANY OF US WERE PARENTED THROUGH the dysfunctional model of punishment and shame. Whenever we would express ourselves out of turn (tantrums, outbursts, etc.), refuse to finish everything on our plate, fight with a sibling, or act out, we may have been shamed for our actions, sent to our rooms to be alone, and reprimanded for being "bad." Some of us were also physically punished through spanking or hitting. Attachment theory has taught us that using these control tactics to teach children lessons greatly damages their self-esteem—and can even amplify behavioral issues. Sensitive kids act out with aggression, and it only escalates the more they are punished, told they are bad, or separated from the rest of the group.

Punishment and humiliation don't teach us how to be better people; they teach us that something about us is not okay, and we learn to internalize, rebel, self-reject, or put on a mask to fit in. They teach us that we cannot trust our caregivers and the bond is broken, forcing us to look to the outside world for approval. As adults, a lot of us still carry on these patterns through self-harming behaviors like talking down to ourselves, making little room for failure, ignoring our body and our needs for rest and compassion, or projecting our mistrust and fear of control onto others.

Change does not happen through criticism, judgment, and self-blame but through connection, encouragement, and praise. As long as we are running on a story that we're broken or not good enough we cannot heal, because at the root of our patterns is the belief that we deserve to suffer. The key to self-acceptance is to approach our patterns with compassionate self-awareness—so that we can grow, take responsibility for our lives, and begin to live in alignment with our hearts, not only for ourselves, but also for our families and communities.

Think back to some of the ways you were conditioned to silence your voice, mute your power, or people please. You may have been told you were a problem, too sensitive, too loud, or too shy; you may have even taken on some of these external labels as the truth of your identity. There comes a time when we must take a sincere look at what internal dialogue we've been carrying around with us and shed all the noise so we can embody our gifts for the world.

As you begin to unpack your patterns, you may recognize ways you show up inauthentically in your relationships, a habit learned long ago as a way to self-protect. Rather than judge yourself, get curious about who you are underneath the mask. When we approach our patterns with curiosity we will almost always find that all the choices we have made have been rooted in a desire for love, connection, or safety, and how can we make ourselves wrong for that?

Now, your work is to unwind your conditioning by taking ownership over your life and how you show up in the world. As you embark down this road of self-knowledge, there are three tools to bring with you: self-compassion, self-acceptance, and self-forgiveness.

Self-Compassion

Creating a kind and loving internal dialogue is the foundation of self-compassion. When we are in self-rejection, we talk down to ourselves and hold ourselves to an impossible standard of perfection. Self-compassion can look like giving ourselves time to rest and taking care to reframe our negative self-judgments into more loving and accepting thoughts.

Self-Acceptance

Part of being human is knowing that we have the capacity to do both good and evil. Self-acceptance does not mean enabling behaviors that are harmful or throwing our hands up instead of taking action to make real change, but instead making room for all parts of ourselves to be there. In the absence of shame, we can bring more honesty to our process. Only then can we step into our authenticity and let down our defenses.

Self-Forgiveness

When you confront an aspect of your past behavior or your role in a pattern, your biggest opportunity for transformation lies in your ability to be gentle with yourself. Notice how your body feels when you're taking ownership over your patterns. If you feel tension, tightness, shame, heat, or another sensation that feels uncomfortable, it's okay to slow down, return to your breath, and speak loving thoughts to yourself. A good mantra to recite is "You're safe, you're okay, and I forgive you."

IGNORING OUR INNER MESSENGER

When I was nineteen years old, I sat down on my new boyfriend's couch. For the sake of this story, let's call him Sean. He had just spoken to me in a very aggressive tone, and the energy he was emitting was mean and jarring. As I looked out the window into the parking lot outside of his apartment unit, the message that came in was loud and clear: "This person is unsafe, and he's going to become abusive." But rather than get up and leave, or break up with Sean, I moved in with him and continued on for about a year. He did become abusive, and he was, in fact, incredibly unsafe.

What is it that drives us to ignore our inner messenger, and how do we forgive ourselves for not listening? You may be able to think of one or many instances where you ignored your intuition, didn't listen to the little whispers or giant pangs of your body that something was off. Maybe you have justified harmful behavior or spent too long trying to help someone see the light, when in reality, you were putting yourself at risk.

For years after that relationship ended, I was incredibly hard on myself for not trusting my intuition. Self-judgment and regret held me in a cycle of shame. It was only when I was able to find compassion for myself and what was under my impulse to ignore my intuition that I began to shift.

Most of us have ignored our intuition or dismissed signs that something wasn't right, and one of the hardest parts of the healing process can be finding compassion for ourselves. We might think we know how we'll react or respond when we're under threat or faced with conflict, but the truth is, we don't really know until we get there, and a lot of times, when survival mode kicks in, we react in ways we never thought we would. We may deny, numb out, freeze, attack back, cling, or, in some cases, run. But a lot of times, our own reactions surprise us. Sometimes, we miss the signs entirely, but that doesn't mean our intuition is broken or that we can never trust ourselves again. Perhaps the other person may have unconsciously felt similar to someone from your childhood but "different enough" that you hoped this time you'd be able to get your needs met.

When an unhealed part of ourselves is at the wheel, our subconscious mind is so focused on closing an open loop that we tend to ignore or justify when something feels off. Find empathy for the part of you that wanted to be loved, the part of you that wanted to heal.

OWNING YOUR PART IN THE PATTERN

My dynamic with Sean was one of rage, insecurity, and chaos. All my hidden defenses came to the surface, and while I wasn't responsible for his actions, I contributed to the dynamic with my own uncalibrated anger and emotionally immature reactions. Rather than looking inward, the relationship we cocreated was an extension of both of our wounds being hurled at one another.

Eventually there comes a time in the healing process when we must turn inward to confront the ways we may be unconsciously perpetuating a pattern or dynamic.

One of the main concerns I get from folks whenever I address accountability work in my programs is that it feels like self-blame or makes them feel as if it's all their fault that their relationships haven't worked out or that someone hurt them. This is not at all in alignment with the true essence of accountability work.

Taking ownership of our patterns doesn't mean that we're here "to blame"; it means that we're ready to wake up and take control of our lives. That we no longer choose to see ourselves as helpless, and instead, that we're ready to embody our fire, our power. It means that we're willing to look behind the curtain and pause for long enough to see how we might be playing out old stories in our relationships that really need to die so we can transform. It also means being accountable for our mind, our judgments, our angry thoughts, and the ways we blame, project, criticize, or complain instead of creating change in our lives, speaking directly to our fears/wants/needs, or setting a boundary.

True accountability work must be paired with self-compassion to be effective. When we own our part from a place of acceptance, that is when doors open to deeper self-awareness. Healing doesn't mean erasing your past and trying to become a completely different person; it means acknowledging the things that have been silently dominating your life so you can do better the next time around.

OUR PATTERNS CHANGE WHEN WE DO

Many of us resist doing accountability work because it's so confronting and often brings with it a spiral of shame and self-judgment. But it's possible to take responsibility for our part in the pattern from a place of self-love and witness ourselves as though we are a loving parent raising an innocent child.

While taking ownership for your mind, emotions, and behaviors might sting at times, the gift is that you are rightfully returned to a position of authority in your life. If we don't take ownership for our patterns, we may feel temporary comfort wrapped in a blanket of blissful ignorance, but that also means we are destined to run on the same loop—believing if only we can find the right person, things will change. Things don't change until we do—and knowing that we have a part in our relationship patterns means we have the ability to change them.

This work is vital to anyone who wishes to be a conscious partner, a caring friend, and an integrated human being in their community. It isn't easy to admit that sometimes we may be the ones who are overly critical, harsh, aggressive, dismissive, avoidant, controlling, domineering, defensive, or hurtful. It's equally challenging to forgive ourselves for welcoming unsafe people into our lives.

But the truth is we all have the capacity to cause pain and heartache—every single one of us. We cannot hold ourselves in purgatory forever; we must gather our lessons and try again.

Tend to your emotional body with kindness as you uncover aspects of your personality that may have been hiding in the shadows, and remember that taking ownership does not mean you are a bad person. Self-awareness is how we step into confidence, emotional maturity, and leadership in our lives and within our communities.

SHINING A LIGHT WITHIN

Within each of us, there are parts of ourselves we'd rather deny or cover up because we believe they're unlovable, unattractive, or threatening to our survival. Our emotional programming is an aspect of this repression. We take cues from the world around us about what's acceptable and what's not, and we conform to those standards, distancing ourselves from certain sides of our personality. As a result, we tend to relegate the parts of ourself we're least in touch with to the basement of our mind.

When we're entirely disconnected from our own rejected parts, they come out sideways, wreaking havoc on our relationships and causing us to feel embarrassed when they unexpectedly surface. We may get stuck in reactionary mode, responding to our big emotions from an immature or wounded place, lashing out at others or the world around us, unable to cope with the intensity that arises within us.

With accountability work and self-awareness, we can see what lies within and become more emotionally grounded, freeing us to navigate the world in a more harmonious way. This also allows us to witness our inner perfectionist in moments of stress and overwhelm with more compassion. One step at a time, we shift into a more relaxed state of being and become at peace with who we are.

HEALING OUR INNER PERFECTIONIST

Years ago, in one of my women's circles, there was a woman named Mina. Mina had a strong perfectionist streak that prevented her from taking risks and expressing herself because she was too afraid of getting something wrong. Her signature look included square-framed glasses and a tight and orderly bun on top of her head, a reflection of her internal need to keep things tidy and organized. Mina struggled with anxiety and rarely took up space, even when invited to do so. As a group, we expressed to Mina that we desired to see her energy unbound and challenged her to let her hair down. Naturally, this was a challenge for her, but slowly, we watched Mina transform, first with her hair down, and then with her energy more relaxed. Her anxiety lessened, and she began to use her voice more in group. Today, Mina is in a leadership position and co-facilitating women's circles.

Perfectionism is not the same as being ambitious or a "high achiever." Perfectionism is an exhausting pursuit that never ends because we are under the belief that nothing we do is ever good enough and we are constantly overwhelmed by a fear of failure. The fear says, "If I fail, I'm not worthy of love." This all-consuming pattern of leaving behind our needs and desires to prioritize the approval, praise, or validation of others is a form self-abandonment. Perfectionism can also be projected outward in our relationships, leading us to be highly critical and put a lot of pressure on our significant others to measure up to an impossible standard.

Freeing ourselves from perfectionism is vital to living a life of joy and creativity, which is all about taking risks and being open to the possibilities of life. We can't walk through a door to the unknown if we're confining ourselves and others to rigid and unattainable standards.

SIGNS OF PERFECTIONISM

- Being hypercritical of self and others
- Defending against love and closeness by creating problems
- Struggling to celebrate your own achievements or wins because you believe they're not good enough
- Feeling like you'll never measure up
- Comparing yourself to and competing with others
- Feeling constant pressure to perform, do more, be better
- Struggling to rest, slow down, relax, and surrender

At the heart of any *perfectionist wound* is often a fear that if we slow down or let go of control, we might have to feel something we've been avoiding or discover that our worst fears about ourselves are true. Perfectionists can be deeply self-critical, but can also defend themselves from intimacy and deep connection by being overly critical of others, saying, in effect, "If there's always something to pick apart, then I don't have to get too close to you and risk being hurt." It takes such courage to admit that we may be responsible for keeping love at a distance or even sabotaging our relationships.

If you see yourself in the perfectionism wound, this is an invitation to take a breath and let yourself be the beautifully imperfect and wonderful human that you are. Life isn't meant to be controlled and neatly organized. We need to slow down and be willing to allow our true selves to come forward, without self-judgment or impossible standards.

WAYS TO PRACTICE LETTING GO OF PERFECTIONISM

- Try letting your house be a little messy when someone comes over.

- Make the art, write the post, or share the unformulated, imperfect creation.

- Dance uninhibited to music you love.

- Remind yourself it's okay to make mistakes.

- Give yourself permission to have feelings like rage, anger, hate, and sadness without judgment.

- Ask a friend to help cook dinner if you're hosting a gathering rather than trying to do it all yourself.

- Listen to your body and make space for rest days and emotional ups and downs.

- Do something a little bit different with your routine, even if it's letting your hair down like Mina did, or trying a new outfit that feels exciting and a little bit edgy for you.

HOW TO DO
ACCOUNTABILITY WORK

Becoming accountable for your patterns requires noticing when you judge, criticize, or blame others and then pausing to ask yourself, *What am I avoiding in myself by focusing externally?* When you feel jealousy, anger, or self-pity, consider what core fear lies underneath this feeling. Being conscious is learning to bridge the connection between your head and your heart. If your mind is racing or you start to feel discomfort or body tension, slow down and find your breath so you don't project the energy outward and can instead self-regulate and own your experience.

As we shine a light inward, our homing beacon should always be self-acceptance so that we can integrate all the qualities that make up who we are. With nothing to mask or defend, we naturally soften and become more available for this dance called life.

Journaling Session: Accountability Work

Grab your journal and a pen and give yourself some time to be with your thoughts, fears, and feelings. Answer the questions below, giving yourself grace and compassion through the process. Know that it's not only okay, *it's healthy* to experience big emotions as you dive into yourself and open old wounds in order to heal. You're safe.

- What is your default emotion in conflict (e.g., anger, sadness, fear, anxiety)?

- How do you tend to express yourself when you're upset (e.g., yelling, attacking, blaming, shaming, over-apologizing, shutting down)?

- What emotion are you the most afraid of in others?

- What judgments do you have about that emotion?

- Do you let yourself express or feel that emotion? When you do, what happens?

- Are there any recurring feelings from childhood that seem to pop up in your adult relationships (e.g., feeling unheard, unseen, powerless, abandoned)?

- What traits or characteristics repulse you the most in other people (e.g., greed, jealousy, anger, boastfulness, arrogance)?

- Do you see those characteristics in yourself at all? (Dive deep here; an ounce of ownership can go a long way!)

- If yes, write a bit about how that characteristic or trait shows up in your own expression.

- What sides of yourself do you show when you're the most comfortable with someone or with your closest friends (e.g., silly, expressive, serious)?

- What do people assume about you that feels hurtful?

- What do you wish people saw in you?

- How could you practice embodying more of that now?

- What emotion would you like to learn how to be more comfortable with?

- What is a habit or pattern of behavior you are ready to shift?

No one heals their patterns by journaling alone; this process is designed to help you feel more connected to yourself and understand what's going on beneath the surface of your reactions and defenses. You don't need to "do" anything with this information other than allow it to bring you more self-awareness and invite you into a state of deeper compassion for yourself.

SHARING YOUR PROCESS WITH OTHERS

A lot of the women I've worked with feel overcome when they finally integrate what it means to be accountable for their patterns. It's common to want to reach out to an ex from the past to share everything they've learned. While it might be tempting to share your revelations with an ex-partner, it's not usually recommended, especially if the relationship was tumultuous or they were abusive in some way. Your accountability work is vulnerable and sacred, and you don't need to share anything with people who have hurt you to take ownership and move forward. If you're in a relationship now, then you may want to share what you discover with your current partner, but be sure to do it with context, and be prepared for anything.

As a guideline, I suggest you hold off on sharing an intimate process of your inner work until you've really integrated it, or until you can share it without needing validation. Your loved ones may or may not reward you for sharing so vulnerably, and it's also possible you'll get a response you really don't like. For this reason, I suggest keeping your process close to your heart and only sharing with people you know you can trust and who have some foundation for this work, like a therapist, coach, spiritual guide, friend, or partner—provided they have shown you that they can hold a loving space for your vulnerability, or you're willing to take responsibility for whatever arises in you if you don't get the response you wanted.

SELF-COMPASSION
MOMENT TO MOMENT

Adopting a more compassionate mind-set when we have a low moment or revert to an old familiar coping mechanism can make all the difference in whether being self-aware feels sustainable or not. In moments where you react in ways that bring up shame or guilt, remember that perfection is not the goal. Speak to yourself with the warmth you would give to an innocent and precious child.

Self-Compassion in Action Practice

Place a hand on your heart and a hand on your belly and take a few long, slow, deep breaths. Try a box breath: inhale for four counts, hold for four counts, exhale for four counts. Now, how can you soften your internal dialogue? What supportive, kind, and loving words do you need to hear right now? You can also try expanding on the following sentences in a journal:

Even though I reacted by _____, I am still a good person.

Even though right now I am feeling _____, I am worthy of love.

Even though right now I am feeling _____, I can access other feelings underneath like _____ and _____.

I am proud of myself for _____.

THINGS TO REMEMBER

- Self-judgment and shame can keep us stuck in our patterns. The key to moving forward is through compassionate self-awareness.

- A lot of our rejected parts were hidden in order to survive, win love, and gain approval. By bringing compassion and acceptance to these parts of ourselves, we shift how we relate to our patterns and reclaim our wholeness.

- Being accountable means playing an active role in your life and your relationships rather than being an innocent bystander.

- Accountability work is not about blaming yourself; it's about having the power to show up more consciously.

- Accountability work can be liberating because, at the root, the purpose of it all is self-acceptance!

- Self-awareness clears the path for deeper transformation to occur.

- Nobody is perfect; it's okay to make mistakes.

Your body is sacred.
Your energy is sacred.
Choose your lovers
and friends wisely.
This life is too precious
to be wasted
on those who wish
to keep you small.

CHAPTER 11

RED FLAGS, GREEN FLAGS

IF ONLY LIFE WERE AS EASY AS BREAKING DOWN behaviors into simple and concise little lists. All we'd need on a date is a checklist and voilà—no more relationship dysfunction! But life cannot be broken down into tidy lists, and recognizing red flags requires a lot more nuance than checking off boxes. In this chapter, we're going to break down red, yellow, and green flags in detail. However, rather than spending the majority of our time on red flags, we're going to focus on what green flags look like.

Think about it: If we're always on the lookout for red flags, what are we calling in? Exactly, *more* of the same. Is that the type of energy you want to bring with you each time you meet someone or go on a date? It's more powerful to lay a foundation for what healthy and happy relationships look and feel like, so you can normalize green flags and expect nothing less from the people you interact with. I'm also going to cover how to tell the difference between a true red flag, and a false alarm; in other words, is it fear or intuition?

To some extent, there are universally agreed-upon red flags like abuse and violence. However, you may find certain things on the yellow flags list that you feel should be on the red flags list, like lying or cheating. There are going to be things that remain subjective to you, your core values, and your circumstances.

Just one hundred years ago, divorce was incredibly taboo; most couples were married after a very short courtship, and then stayed together even if they were unhappy. Now, we've swung to the other end of the pendulum, where we're quick to exit a relationship and less likely to lean in when things get hard. But there is no perfect person out there who is going to meet all of your needs 100 percent of the time. We are all going to hurt and be hurt in a relationship, and it's important to know when to walk away, and when it's time to roll up our sleeves and do the work. No one else can tell you what is right for you and your relationship—that is up to you. Generally, if you are in a relationship and there is mutual love, respect, attraction, and a willingness to do the work together, then progress can be made. If one or both of you doesn't want to repair, or doesn't see the harm in their actions, you're on a hamster wheel going nowhere.

I don't like to put definitive boxes around all mishaps and breakdowns that can occur in a relationship, because we all make mistakes and sometimes those moments birth opportunities for healing and understanding between two people. Other times, they are opportunities for you to find your fire, set a firm boundary, and exit the relationship. Some boundary violations are too serious or too close to home for second chances. If your body is saying no, listen to that. You never have to stay in a situation that feels unsafe in the name of "doing the work." Sometimes doing the work looks like walking away.

WHAT ARE RED, YELLOW, AND GREEN FLAGS?

While oversimplified, red, yellow, and green flags help us break down behavior into categories: Red is unacceptable and possibly even dangerous, yellow is a warning to pay attention because something may need adjustment, and green is a healthy and connected relationship.

While at times categorizing and labeling everything can become dogmatic or limiting, sometimes categories help us when we're uncertain or confused about what's okay and what's not. I've done my best here to expand on the concept of red, yellow, and green flags so you have more clarity moving forward, but if you're ever unsure, it's always useful to seek out professional guidance from someone you trust—whether that's a licensed therapist, a spiritual counselor, a coach, or a guide.

RED FLAGS

Red flags are generally deal breakers. They are characteristics or behaviors that require serious repair, attention, or resolution before a healthy relationship can happen. Many of us have normalized red flag behavior due to our early exposure to abuse, neglect, or dysfunction. If we see ourselves in the red flags list, then it's up to us to take action to repair any harm done and do the work necessary to shift our behavior.

SIGNS OF RED FLAGS

- They use abusive language when speaking about their ex or their family members.

- When they talk about their past relationships, their exes all happen to be crazy or psycho.

- They show anger or aggression toward strangers, people in the service industry, or drivers on the road.

- They have an active addiction to substances or engage in risky behavior.

- Their behavior is controlling, attempting to put a wedge between you and your loved ones.

- You feel unsafe expressing yourself or disagreeing for fear of retaliation.

- They push your boundaries or ignore you when you say "no" and think it's funny.

- They show jealous and suspicious behavior and violate your personal privacy by going through your devices or journals.

- The climate of the relationship is one of tension and confusion. It feels like a roller coaster, and you never know what they're going to do next or where you stand.

- They show rude or insensitive sexual behavior, making hurtful comments about your body.

- Your relationship is "secret," and you haven't met any of their friends or family members.

- Your conflicts are explosive, and they never apologize (ever).

- They dodge any attempts you make to talk about the relationship, they put you down, or they say you're too difficult or too much work.

- Literally no one in your life likes the person you're dating (like no one at all).

- They make sexual comments about your close friends or flirt with other people in front of you.

- They turn into a different person when they drink and it makes you feel unsafe, but they don't think it's a problem.

- When the honeymoon phase wears off, they are entirely different.

- They have a mental illness that causes pain for everyone, but they refuse to get help.

- Your relationship is full of red flags, but they refuse to acknowledge the issues and aren't interested in doing the work.

- You can't explain it, but you just feel off, uncomfortable, or unsafe in their presence.

YELLOW FLAGS

Yellow flags are like warning signs inviting you to pay attention and ask questions. They usually indicate that it's wise to proceed with caution. In real life, virtually all relationships are going to have some yellow flags. It's highly unlikely that both you and your potential partner are going to have everything figured out by the time you cross paths. A yellow flag is an opportunity to have clear and direct conversations and find out what each of you is willing to work on or whether there is resistance to growth. A yellow flag can turn into a red flag if these conversations are met with denial or resistance, but they can turn into a green flag if they lead to more honesty and a new commitment to transform what is out of alignment in the relationship.

SIGNS OF YELLOW FLAGS

- One or both of you are keeping secrets or lying.

- Your family and friends strongly dislike the person. They say they're worried or concerned for you.

- You can't talk about your feelings or have vulnerable discussions.

- They're in piles of debt and there's no good explanation for it.

- They don't like to answer questions and say things like "leave the past in the past."

- They are consistently unemployed, getting fired, or asking to borrow money.

- They cancel on you at the last minute.

- They don't have any personal hobbies, interests, or passions.

- They have a history of infidelity.

- They don't post or share anything about your relationship on social media (if they are active social media users).

- They become easily frustrated during conflict or struggle to communicate their emotions.

- They are still communicating with their exes. This is a nuanced one, because in some cases, this can actually be a green flag! A person who has a friendship with an ex can be positive and demonstrate their relational skills. It becomes a yellow or a red flag when there are secrets, you're excluded, you have never met the person and you're not welcome to do so, or the ex is crossing boundaries by not respecting your relationship.

GREEN FLAGS

Green flags mean go! In the context of a relationship, a green flag is a sign that both partners are operating from a place of mutual respect, authenticity, trust, and appreciation. When we're in a green flag relationship, there's a sense of safety and security. We know we can be ourselves and have our own thoughts, opinions, and desires.

SIGNS OF GREEN FLAGS

- You feel safe to express yourself openly.
- A disagreement doesn't threaten the relationship.
- Friendships and family connections outside of the romantic relationship are encouraged.
- Boundaries around physical touch, sexuality, communication, and personal belongings are respected.
- Each person is responsible for their energy/emotions and behavior.
- In conflict, both of you are accountable for how you show up rather than one person "always" or "never" being "right."
- The relationship inspires you to be your best self, and to shine love into the world.
- When times are hard or stress hits, you are both willing to lean in or give each other space rather than withholding love or punishing each other.
- The climate of the relationship is consistent, not chaotic.
- You lift each other up in front of others, and there's no belittling or put-downs.

- You can be vulnerable with one another without worrying that it will be used against you.

- Conflicts are spaces where growth can occur, not where harm is inflicted verbally or physically.

- You can repair after conflict.

- You're both able to sit down and discuss the disagreement afterward, and work toward showing up better for one another.

- You both have a life outside of the relationship.

- The relationship is a source of inspiration for you both.

WHAT IF THEY ARE WONDERFUL, BUT I STILL DON'T FEEL SAFE?

While there are definitely things a person can do to help their partner feel safe, feeling safe consists of two parts: having a healthy external environment and having a healthy internal environment.

Many of the people I work with describe the utter confusion and disappointment they feel when they meet "someone wonderful" who checks all the boxes and is so loving, kind, and present, and yet, they still don't feel safe! Their mind is still coming up with all sorts of reasons why the partner isn't a good match for them or they're waiting for the other shoe to drop.

It isn't solely on the other person to "make you feel safe"; it's also an inside job. This is why understanding the role your nervous system plays in your relationship patterns is vital to building a new relationship to your body's signals. It helps you understand how you pick up and respond to red, yellow, and green flags; how you express your fears and concerns; and whether you can relax into a safe, secure, and healthy relationship when it arrives.

In addition to the inner work and somatic tools found in this book, practices that get you into your body are the most supportive ways to repattern your system. If you struggle to feel safe, often feel exhausted, or have unresolved traumatic memories, you may wish to expand your tool kit by exploring with a Somatic Experiencing Practitioner. Working with the nervous system, while subtle, can move the needle in a powerful way. Combine nervous system healing with inner work to help the body catch up to all the repatterning your mind is doing. This is what gives us the power to heal.

WHAT IF ALL I KNOW ARE
RED FLAG RELATIONSHIPS?

Some of us have only known red flag relationships, and until we have the foundation to experience something different, we may not believe green flag relationships are within reach. I empathize with those who worry that they're just too broken to have a healthy relationship, because I've had those thoughts myself. With commitment, it's absolutely possible to step outside of those ingrained patterns and create a conscious relationship. More than that, it's possible for you to experience a complete metamorphosis, from how you relate to the world at large, to how you show up for work, to how you connect with your family, friendship circles, community, and more.

The inner work has so many benefits, and I've seen thousands of people thrive who come from some of the most painful and traumatic pasts—not always in spite of their past, but often because of it. Sometimes our painful history provides us with a doorway to meet ourselves so deeply that, in the end, what is left is a well of wisdom, love, and compassion. Without diminishing the reality of how incredibly hard it is when you've experienced trauma, what you've been through has given you the gift of being more empathic and understanding.

CAN A RED FLAG RELATIONSHIP TURN INTO A CONSCIOUS RELATIONSHIP?

Anyone who's been in a red flag relationship knows how disorienting it can be. When we're in it, it can be hard to see just how unhealthy the pattern is. Often, it isn't until we've stepped away from the relationship that it all starts to hit us. We find ourselves questioning how and why we stayed for so long or why we allowed that behavior to continue.

One of the most common questions I get when I'm working with groups and the subject of red flags comes up is, "Can a red flag relationship turn into a conscious relationship?" The answer to that isn't a simple one.

On one hand, if there is mutual love and willingness, almost any pattern in a relationship can shift. On the other hand, when two people want to shift a red flag relationship into something safe and secure, the relationship in its current form has to die completely. In essence, you may be able to shift the relationship only if you are both ready and willing to rebuild from the ground up. Often in a red flag relationship, the willingness just isn't there. Usually, one partner is willing, and the other isn't, and in that scenario, the only way to transform the pattern is to step out of the dynamic and do the work solo.

CAN A RED FLAG RELATIONSHIP BE A SOUL MATE OR A TWIN FLAME?

It's certainly possible that a person you're in a turbulent relationship with is a soul mate or a twin flame. Even if they are, it is not a reason to stay in a red flag relationship, nor does it mean that you're destined to be together.

Personally, I believe we have many soul mates in this life—not just one or two but more than a hundred people that our souls travel with. Some of our soul mates will be close friends, family members, lovers, and even pets, but some may not be in our inner circle at all. The person you see at the grocery store frequently or who delivered your mail for the past fifteen years could also be in your soul cluster. The idea that we only have one soul mate—the mythical "one"—can create a mind-set of scarcity and lead us to hang on to something that isn't good for us. A spiritual connection is never an excuse to self-abandon. So while you may or may not be encountering a soul mate type of relationship, trust that it's okay to let go when necessary.

HOW TO KNOW WHETHER IT'S FEAR OR INTUITION

Our intuition can often be muddled by our stories. If we have unhealed relationships or triggers from the past, our mind might become very good at building evidence around our greatest fears in relationships: being dismissed, controlled, feeling insignificant, being hurt, and so on. One of the most powerful things you can do to train your intuition is get to know how your mind operates and how your wounds and fears manifest. With clarity and accountability, you can trust your body when it speaks to you.

Fear is often combined with a lot of mental chatter and "story-telling" or predictions of catastrophes. Intuition is an "instinctual" sense, an "inner knowing." It's more a subtle whisper than a frantic demand. When we're being run by a fear, we'll usually revert to our ego fantasy—you'll recall mine was to run away and live all alone in the forest. When it's our intuition, we may be called to take action, but toward something that serves our highest good. Our fears and projections can block us from this authentic connection, leading our minds to make up a list of worst-case scenarios or come up with judgments. A healthy connection to our inner voice is only truly possible when we're seeing the world through a clean lens. Learning to trust our intuition involves challenging our mind and our body when we receive a message so that we can be confident our choices come from truth and not our past conditioning.

THROWN INTO THE DEEP END

In true power-struggle fashion, as soon as Ben and I committed to deepening our relationship by getting married, all of my fears rose to the surface in full glory. I spent the majority of our one-plus-year engagement swimming in my own ego drama.

Looking back, I have so much compassion for the little girl in me that was terrified of being betrayed, disrespected, or taken advantage of. Not only was that my childhood history, but I had also experienced it in my divorce and was about to go into a second marriage. It felt like such a huge risk to be taking, and the truth is, I almost backed out many times. My shame around having a "second marriage" and the potential reality that maybe this one wouldn't work out either were a constant presence in my mind. During that time, I pushed Ben away, hard. We argued and fought more than we ever had before, and I even tried canceling the wedding. Fortunately, Ben and I both had the tools and a strong enough foundation together to ride the waves, but it was very difficult.

One day, Ben and I were packing our house to move, and he said something to me in a way that felt aloof and dismissive. Instead of breathing through it and recognizing that we were both stressed, I instantly spiraled. I retreated to our bedroom and sat in the closet. I knew that I needed support, so I called my dear friend and relationship coach Jordan Gray. He made room for me to vent my frustrations and fears. "I'm afraid that Ben is going to try to control me, that he's not going to respect me, that he won't even see me, he'll just bulldoze me, and I'll disappear," I said to him through the hot tears streaming down my face. He took a moment to really listen to what I was saying, and then gently responded, "Well, it seems like since you've been in a relationship with Ben, you've only become more empowered and more visible, don't you think?" Instantly, my state changed. It was like he woke me up from a dream. "Yes, that's true," I said. "Thank you, I was really in it there."

Jordan was able to see where I was at, and without judgment or colluding with my fears, gently help me move back into reality, into my present relationship. That's the power of friendships with other people who are also devoted to the inner work.

Choose Your Friends Wisely

Having trusted friends or confidantes who are willing to challenge you when needed is vital. In conventional friendship dynamics, it's customary to collude with each other and talk smack about an ex or take sides when a friend is in a fight with their partner. Everyone needs to feel supported, and sometimes what we need most is just to feel validated in our experience. But at other times, this can be destructive. In a conscious friendship, the role of a friend is to listen, be curious, and potentially reflect things back that will allow for introspection and healing to occur. Just like Jordan gently woke me up when I was projecting onto Ben, we all want at least one friend, or a trusted therapist, coach, or guide, whom we can count on to help us when we're in a state of confusion.

TO TAKE ACTION OR QUIET THE FEAR

Regardless of whether it's your fear or intuition speaking, if something doesn't feel right, you should never ignore that. Being in tune with your fears means acknowledging them, not dismissing them. Sometimes there's a valid reason for fear coming up, and sometimes fear is just the natural response to change on the horizon. We're creatures of comfort, after all, so we can expect that when we make big moves in our lives, we'll have to ride a few waves of discomfort. This even applies to some of the happiest milestones too—things like starting a new relationship, getting engaged, getting married, purchasing a home, having a child, getting the promotion you've always wanted, or accomplishing one of your biggest goals can bring unexpected fears to the surface, but that doesn't mean something is wrong!

Our fears are sacred. Honoring them is a vulnerable process that deserves our loving awareness. What we want to avoid is reacting to our fears as if they are absolute truth, and instead, move into a space of self-inquiry, patience, and curiosity when they arise.

Moving toward your fears consciously gives you an opportunity to resolve whatever wound is being activated. When you also choose to share your internal world with those you care for, you offer them a chance to heal with you. On the flip side, if your fear is pointing toward the reality that this person or relationship isn't aligned for you, you can practice being direct and asking the clarifying questions you need to ask.

WHEN A FEAR ARISES, FOLLOW THIS PROCESS

Acknowledge the fear.

Ask yourself where this fear is coming from—is it from a past experience? Is there a solid basis for this fear, is it being rooted in the reality of this relationship, or does it feel old?

Locate the fear.

Where do you feel this fear in your body? Does your body have words for you? Remember, the body can also be conditioned to respond a certain way, so challenge your body a bit. Ask, "Is this coming from clarity or conditioning?"

Test the fear.

Ask your fear, "What is the worst thing that could happen? And then what?" Keep going until you get to the root of the fear itself.

Reveal your fear.

If it feels right to do so, you can invite the person with whom your fears are arising to hold space for you and share what's coming up. You can also do mirror work and reveal the fear to yourself by facing a mirror and sharing from your heart.

Release your fear.

You may choose to put an object on your altar that represents this fear and its lesson for you at this time, or write a letter to burn on the next moon cycle. When you're ready, you can do something ritualistic to symbolize releasing the fear from your life, such as a flower bath, a burning ritual, or giving the object back to nature (only use natural and responsibly harvested items for this like leaves, pine cones, stones, flowers, or soil).

SEEING THROUGH FALSE ALARMS

When we are conditioned to expect the worst, we may cut and run, or make assumptions and catastrophize before we have enough information.

Yes, there are obvious red flags that make it justified to turn around and walk immediately. Abusive situations don't require you to gain more clarity on their intent, but I'm talking about something different here. What I'm talking about is projecting our fears into a relationship that has its normal ups and downs and catastrophizing over little things. It's presuming a new partner is seeing someone else because you saw them on a dating app although you've just begun dating, or labeling them as emotionally unavailable or avoidant if they don't immediately fall in love with your cat.

When we've experienced a lot of pain and trauma in past relationships, it makes sense that we will be extra cautious, and this can be wise. But we also have to be willing to be direct and communicate clearly so we can give people a chance to share their reality with us. Someone with an abandonment wound can spiral pretty hard over a fairly minor misunderstanding and make it mean something really negative. When the abandonment wound is activated, the mind will drum up all sorts of potential stories, often very bleak in nature.

In these moments, you might be responding to a false alarm rather than a real red flag. You may be giving in to familiar fears that are not aligned with reality: *They don't care, they aren't into me, they're a bad person, they will leave, they are avoidant, they are untrustworthy,* and so on. Moments like these are great opportunities to "test" the relationship or potential relationship by showing up as a mature adult, asking clarifying questions, and sharing what you desire. How people respond in these moments will bring a lot more clarity than what your mind can make up on its own.

DOING REALITY CHECKS:
HOW TO ASK FOR CLARITY

If you have ever watched a romantic comedy, then you know the primary way the writers create tension is by having two people who have good intentions very badly misunderstand each other and then refuse to communicate directly, leading to chaos, frustration, and games. Direct communication and giving people a chance to show up for you can save a lot of mental gymnastics.

You become empowered by learning how to communicate directly, be curious, and practice relating to others in a new way. This means that instead of making assumptions or leaping to judgment, you slow down and take a breath. When you're centered, you can approach the person to initiate a conversation. Doing a "reality check" means noticing when your ego/mind is spinning out or crafting a story, and pausing long enough to verify whether that story is true or false.

Now if you're on a first date and someone is giving you the creeps, you don't need to process that with them. There's no need to have a reality check with another person unless you want to give the relationship a chance. But in cases like mine, where I was about to marry someone and my mind was going haywire on me, a reality check was exactly what I needed to wake up out of the haze I was in and come back to my center.

A reality check helps you decipher fear from intuition. It requires being courageous and willing to communicate. You may not always get the answer you want, but you will get clarity, and that's what matters most. Sometimes we don't ask questions because, deep down, we don't really want the answer. We're afraid to let go, so we ignore red flags, or we don't question them until everything falls apart or blows up in our face.

There's another potential reality that's made possible through communication, and that's a richer sense of intimacy and understanding in the relationship. Our minds are always making up meaning or telling us stories, but sometimes the meaning we make isn't correct. Sometimes, we're really just in one of those romantic comedies, where both people have good intentions but aren't being direct.

Choosing When to Share Our Fears

Sharing our fears is incredibly vulnerable, and while the inner work requires that we take a leap of faith, I also firmly believe that it's fair to be cautious about whom we share our hearts with, especially when we are in a more sensitive stage. Feeling dismissed or rejected when we're just getting our wings in vulnerability isn't ideal. Consider that sometimes you may not be able to bring your fear directly to the person you're triggered by—maybe it's a parent, a person you went on a date with, or even a partner you're in relationship with. Bring your fear to someone you know can hold it for you. If you're not sure, it's always wise to ask for permission before you share. Everyone has their limits. Sometimes we can also process things on our own in a journal or on a walk in the woods.

Doing a Reality Check Can Sound Like This

"I'm processing something heavy right now and I wonder if you have the capacity to hold space for me."

"I have some fears arising in this relationship and I wonder if you would be willing to listen to me without judgment."

"I'm afraid of getting close to you and having my heart broken. I notice myself wanting to run away. I just wanted to say that out loud so the fear doesn't have more power."

"Something you said the other day caused me to spiral, and I want to do a reality check with you. Are you open to that?"

"Something you said brought up emotion for me, and I'm wondering if you'd be open to discussing it with me."

"The other day when you said _____, it brought up _____ for me, because in my history I experienced _____. What did you really mean when you said that?"

"Something that is important to me in a relationship is _____ and I want to know whether that's something you're open to."

THINGS TO REMEMBER

- Red, yellow, and green flags require nuance; we cannot oversimplify this topic.

- Red flags are nonnegotiable deal breakers, but those can look slightly different to each of us.

- Some red flags like abuse should never be tolerated, whereas something like infidelity may be something a couple chooses to work through together. Honor yourself in this process.

- We all make mistakes and show up in messy ways sometimes. The most important thing is that you take accountability for yourself and commit to your healing process.

- When we've been hurt or betrayed in the past, we might experience "false alarms" and be quick to cut and run or get anxious. Sometimes we need support from a trusted therapist or guide to help us navigate these situations.

- It's important to focus on picking up green flags and directing your energy toward cultivating healthy and safe relationships.

- The more you honor yourself and commit to self-awareness, the more you will learn to trust your instincts.

PART FOUR

REALIGN WITH YOUR TRUTH

There is a hidden teaching in everything for us if we choose to be open to it. When someone crosses our boundaries, we're being invited to use our voice. When someone avoids intimacy, we're being asked to claim what we truly want in a relationship. Sometimes what looks like rejection is actually a calling into our power.

CHAPTER 12

TRUST YOUR BODY, SET BOUNDARIES

OUR BOUNDARIES ARE AN EXTENSION OF OUR ENERGY and integrity. When someone is overcome by the urge to people please, is known to overfunction, or struggles to say no, we learn to not trust them fully. A person's lack of boundaries may be rooted in the desire to keep love, but instead, it usually turns us off and blocks us from having depth. At their core, our boundaries reflect our openness to life, our relationship to self, and our commitment to honesty.

Boundaries are vital to connection; they strengthen our relationships and create security that comes with knowing we can take a person at their word and trust them to honor their own needs.

The heart of most boundary issues is often a lack of trust in ourself and our body. Developing healthy limits is learning to express ourselves clearly and directly, but it is also just as much about trusting that *we* know what is best for our own emotional, spiritual, and physical well-being.

Setting boundaries with confidence means being willing to say no, let people go, or adjust accordingly when a boundary is continuously crossed. It also means being clear about our intentions—are we creating boundaries to invite a person closer, or to protect ourselves from harmful behavior? Are we setting boundaries from a place of fear, or from a place of love?

If our style of establishing boundaries is not getting us where we want to be, then we can take responsibility and learn to communicate in a new way. When we express ourselves with confidence and self-trust, we can be both kind and firm, direct and mindful in our delivery. With this foundation, we become the authority over our lives, no longer needing to defend our choices. We relax into the truth of who we are and invite in deeper connection with those who mean the most to us.

For a moment, tune inward and imagine what the most radiant and empowered version of yourself would look like. How would it feel to know your worth fully, to trust your yes and your no, to have the capacity to acknowledge what you need, and to set and respect the limits you set for yourself? This chapter and part four of this book is centered around getting crystal clear on your boundaries, what you value most, how you want to be loved, and what you'd like to give and receive in a relationship. We'll also explore your growth edge—the area where you can develop more confidence so that you can communicate exactly what you need.

WHAT ARE BOUNDARIES?

Boundaries are like imaginary lines that separate our physical space, feelings, needs, and responsibilities from others. In their highest form, they allow us to create healthier relationships where we feel seen and respected for who we truly are, and they also let others know what we will and will not accept in terms of behavior and communication.

Boundaries are a dance. If we set them without any flexibility as a way to self-protect, then they can turn into walls that distance us from the connection we crave. If we don't set any at all, then we may find ourselves swimming in a pool of resentment because we haven't prioritized our needs.

The dance is learning to create and honor boundaries in a way that brings us closer to what we want, rather than as a tool for defensiveness. Communicating our needs helps people love us better. Boundaries help us remain in connection with others while also maintaining our sovereignty as individuals. There are also times where we need to set very firm boundaries with people who are consuming, who continue to cross the line. These types of boundaries will have a different flavor—they are meant to create healthy separation.

BOUNDARIES AND OUR SELF-WORTH

Our boundaries are tied to our self-worth. We might feel a sense of dread arise when we think about setting a boundary because we falsely believe that if we define our limits then everyone will leave us, and we'll end up alone. If we are not used to having boundaries, then we may be unsure of what's okay to ask for (which we'll talk about in the next chapter on expectations), where to draw the line between us and "other," and how to set a boundary without pushing love away. If we're really sensitive and empathic, we might carry the belief that it's our job to protect people's feelings. We might not set boundaries because we fear the reaction we might receive. We might even feel reactive or defensive when people set a boundary with us because we interpret it as rejection.

Healing these patterns happens gradually as our sense of self-worth increases and we begin to trust that once we've established our boundaries, only the right people will remain in our lives.

Perhaps you have a rule that you don't want to do dinner on first dates. Maybe you only want to spend time with a certain friend or family member if they aren't drinking. Perhaps you have to say no when a friend asks for your help because you're busy with a project or you simply need rest. Trust that it's okay to say no. Some people may fall away if the energetics of the relationship were hinging on you being needless, but more often than not, people will respect your boundaries and be grateful to you for having them! In some cases, they will even be inspired by you and learn how to set their own. Do your best to surrender to whatever is meant to be—the right people will be there in the end.

THE FIVE TYPES OF BOUNDARIES

PHYSICAL

Physical boundaries are about our personal space and our physical body. When these boundaries are strong, we are aware of our physical limits, preferences, and desires. We respect the boundaries of others by asking for permission before touching them. Many of us experienced the loss of our physical boundaries when we were forced to give hugs as children to people we didn't know. These days, consent is valued much more. Returning to your physical boundaries is about knowing that you have complete domain over your body.

MATERIAL

Material boundaries are about your personal belongings. When your material boundaries are strong, you respect your personal belongings and the belongings of others. This could look like borrowing an item from a friend and returning it exactly when you said you would. Or if someone asks to borrow something and you really don't want to lend it out, you say no. My personal library took quite a hit before I finally changed my boundaries around lending books out.

To those who are sentimental about possessions, material boundaries may hold a lot more weight and require extra care.

EMOTIONAL

Emotional boundaries are about separating our emotions from those of others. They allow us to create an energetic space between us and the other person. Healthy emotional boundaries prevent us from over-giving, taking on blame, emotional rescuing, and feeling responsible for the experience of others. When we have strong emotional boundaries, we can stay in our body and in our own experience while also being able to witness and be present for someone else's experience (without taking it personally). When we have poor emotional boundaries, we may be prone to codependency and enmeshment, where we become absorbed in the other person and every emotion that they have impacts us.

MENTAL

Mental boundaries are about maintaining a sense of self with our thoughts, values, and opinions while also respecting others who may be different from us. When our mental boundaries are poor, we may get reactive when people share opinions that diverge from ours; we may get defensive when we're receiving feedback; or we may adopt other people's judgments as our own. When our mental boundaries are shaky, we feel threatened by differences. We may project and make assumptions rather than adopting an open mind. When we have a healthy level of mental boundaries, we can listen to and receive feedback, hear the opinions of others without immediately taking them on as personal truth, and be curious instead of reactive when someone experiences the world in a contrasting way. We are also able to create a filter to discern what resonates with us and what doesn't while also being flexible enough to change our mind from time to time.

SPIRITUAL

Strong spiritual boundaries mean respecting other people's paths, not interfering or giving unwarranted spiritual advice, and honoring people's energetic bubbles. We all have our own energy bubble, or invisible energy field; some call it an aura. In learning to respect the energetic boundaries of others, we reclaim our sensitivity and slow down so that we can truly sense and feel energy. Honing this skill makes us more compassionate, better listeners, and healthier friends, partners, and community members. With healthy spiritual boundaries, we understand it's not our job to save, fix, or enlighten others.

Spiritual boundaries are very important as we engage in the healing path. We've likely all had the experience of someone else telling us how we should live, grow, or approach our healing, and it can feel intrusive. We know how awful it feels when someone leaps to judgment or assumes they know how we feel or what we believe instead of asking us. When we project our own uninvited beliefs or ideas about how we think others should respond to life, we are in a sense interfering with their destiny. Each of us is here to learn our own lessons and it's not up to us to interrupt that learning process. Good spiritual boundaries allow those of us who are helpers, guides, coaches, or therapists to offer guidance that leaves room for another person's reality to be valid.

BOUNDARY SIGNATURES

Each area of our lives (work, friendship, family, romantic relationship, etc.) has a unique *boundary signature*—whether overly flexible, rigid, or healthy. Most of us struggle with boundaries in some areas and excel in others. We may have healthy boundaries in working relationships, but porous boundaries with our family members and romantic partners. We may have healthy boundaries with most friends, but struggle with boundaries when we're interacting with a person who reminds us of a parent or caretaker from the past.

As you read through the following descriptions, see which boundary signature you relate to most. Each boundary type has a practice to bring you back into balance. Notice how you feel in your body when you read the practice. When the ego senses growth is coming, the protective response is to deflect or resist. If you feel resistance, it could be a sign that leaning into this practice could be transformative for you.

POROUS BOUNDARY SIGNATURE

- Easily influenced by others
- May feel burnt out, bitter, and resentful
- Takes on other people's problems
- Struggles to say no
- Feels like own voice doesn't matter
- Often struggles with an abandonment wound
- Has caretaker or rescuer energy
- Fears rejection or abandonment
- Relies on external validation
- Sees boundaries as mean

Your Practice: You may benefit from embodying the element of fire as we explored in chapter 3 by practicing being confident, direct, and speaking up even if it feels difficult. Your growth edge is to get comfortable putting yourself first and saying no. For a while, you may feel selfish; if so, embrace it. Over time, you'll find a balance between giving and preserving your energy.

RIGID BOUNDARY SIGNATURE

- Stubborn and not open to any influence
- May be defensive rather than curious
- Uses boundaries to shield or guard the heart
- Uses pride to shield emotional vulnerability
- Is unwilling to collaborate
- Is more self-centered than relational

Your Practice: You may benefit from embodying more of the element of water by slowly letting down your walls, connecting with your sensitivity, and letting yourself receive support and love. Your growth edge is to get comfortable being vulnerable and learn to let people in, as well as make room for others' needs and desires. Beneath the hurt and guardedness is a tenderness that is asking for your nurturance.

HEALTHY BOUNDARY SIGNATURE

- Can be firm or flexible when necessary
- Can hear outside opinions or feedback and choose how to respond
- Trusts in the body and inner voice
- Can hold space for other people's pain or emotions without rescuing or caretaking
- Can say no, even if that means feeling some guilt
- Respects other people's boundaries
- Shares personal information in an appropriate manner (no over- or under-sharing)
- Communicates boundaries clearly and directly
- Sees boundaries as a way to create healthier relationships
- Knows self well enough to communicate needs for personal space, time, and so on

Your Practice: There are always areas where our boundaries will be tested. Your growth edge is to continue to be aware when there is an area that needs your attention and trust yourself to communicate in a self-honoring way.

TRUSTING YOUR BODY AND INNER MESSENGER

Your body and your inner messenger—also known as your intuition—are a compass for setting healthy, conscious boundaries. Your inner messenger is not ruled by fear and does not come with stories, but rather is a series of sensations, vibrations, or sounds that help you identify your truth. Our inner messenger contacts each of us differently, and so it's important for you to practice tuning in to your body and learning how it shows up in your own life. Being in tune with your body is the gateway to your power. Your body holds all the medicine and magic for you to heal, find peace, and create the life you want.

HOW OUR INNER MESSENGER MAY SHOW UP

Sensations in the body
Sensations are often messages for when to say yes and no. Sharpness, contraction, a heavy feeling in the gut, or an instant headache is often the body saying no. Tingling, expansion, a light opening, or a "warm" feeling is often the body saying yes.

In the sounds you make
Sounds can often be an indicator of your inner yes or no. If it's in your nature to hem and haw when you make decisions, notice the tone and vibration of the sound you make. Does it feel positively or negatively charged? This inquiry practice can help you be more

attuned to how your body is communicating what does or does not feel good to you. This applies to even the simplest yes or no questions.

A flash of insight

Some of us receive "instant" confirmation. It may happen in the chest, heart, or spleen/kidney area. If you are the type of person to receive "flashes" of insight where you instantly say no, you may be judged as impulsive, or you may not trust the instant knowing and then retreat into your head to argue yourself out of the decision. Your practice is to surrender and trust this insight.

Emotional processing

If you are the type that needs time to make a decision, you may often feel rushed or pressured by others to know right away. Your practice is to honor what you need to make decisions and give yourself time to feel your way to the finish line.

Downloads

Some of us may experience the sensation of an opening in our crown chakra (at the top of our head) with information pouring through. When I receive a download, it's like a tube of light funneling into the top of my head with a message, though others may experience it like something just drops in or lands in the body. Your practice is to spend time nurturing your relationship to Spirit in whatever way resonates, so that you can be open to receiving divine guidance.

COMMUNICATING
OUR BOUNDARIES

For much of our lives, we've been taught to cloak our communication in niceness, but often this leads to indirect communication and avoidance of our true feelings. You can speak directly without being mean, but you also don't need to sugarcoat your words.

The most important part of communicating a boundary is first determining why you have the boundary and what you want to happen by setting it. Energy matters, so being calm and centered in your intention transmits to the person you are in conversation with.

If you are afraid, activated, or angry, that too will transmit. When we're first learning to set healthy boundaries, we may find ourselves swinging from one end of the pendulum to the other. If we're terrified to use our voice, we may puff ourselves up until we snap, or go from having no boundaries to having walls, coming off as aggressive or harsh rather than thoughtful. It can be activating to set boundaries, especially if they've been crossed before. Be tender with yourself when things don't come out the way you intended. If they don't, you can say, "That didn't come out right. Can I try again?"

Before setting a boundary, take a moment to breathe and get into your body. Consider how you want the interaction to go, and connect to the value that's underneath this boundary. It takes time to feel comfortable setting them, and some come more easily than others.

Hold yourself in tenderness as you practice. You won't always get it "perfect," but the important thing to remember is that you're doing your best and you're learning a new skill.

Returning to Your Body Ritual

You can use this ritual before setting a boundary and any time you notice yourself leaving your body. This often happens after a boundary has been crossed, or when we become anxious or overwhelmed.

1. Take three long, deep breaths.
2. Notice your breath. Is it shallow or relaxed?
3. Connect with whatever surface you are on: feel your feet on the ground, your bottom on your seat, your back on the floor or chair.
4. Scan the room, notice where you are, and feel the presence this brings you.
5. Scan your body and notice what sensations you are feeling.
6. Take three more long, deep breaths.
7. Say, "I am present, I am centered, I am safe."

HAVE THE BOUNDARIES TALK FACE-TO-FACE

Millennials and Gen Z text more and talk less—a sign of the times, but also a road to rampant disconnection and a mounting wave of anxiety.

Through text, you cannot hear tone, you can't sense a person's energy or nuance of intended meaning. For this reason, setting boundaries around texting deserves an acknowledgment all its own. So many communication breakdowns occur when we're not communicating directly or we're misinterpreting each other through text.

A good boundary to hold is to communicate anything important, like an inner conflict or a fear that's coming up for you, face-to-face or by telephone if you cannot be in person. If there's hurt feelings, or something that's frustrating you, it's much better to sit with it and request a conversation rather than firing off a paragraph-long text message. Letter writing is another way to communicate, especially if you are still working through somatic tendencies to freeze or shut down when it's time to express a boundary, or if it's really not safe to set one with someone and you don't want to see the person again.

I have written letters to Ben in the past when it was useful for me to get everything out, with the caveat that I checked in first to see whether he would be open to receiving my communication in this way, and there is always a face-to-face conversation that follows. If your boundary setting comes with the intention to strengthen the relationship, gather your courage and have the conversation directly.

BRINGING CLARITY TO YOUR RELATIONSHIPS

When exploring boundary work, we may also want to consider how we express our boundaries.

Are we dancing around the boundary? Are we expressing ourselves clearly and directly? Are we making assumptions, or hoping someone will guess our needs and limits? Do we believe that any decent human being would know our boundaries, and therefore resent them when they do not come through?

It's important to notice how we show up in our relationships and take accountability if we're not setting people up to love us the way we want to be loved. If someone crosses a boundary that we never communicated, it's not fair to punish them or take out our anger on them. It's an opportunity to let them know how they could show up differently. Of course, there are obvious things like not being abusive, name-calling, or engaging in other extreme behaviors that we shouldn't have to lay out in order for people to treat us respectfully. But in most cases, we need to be very straightforward with what we want and need if we are to feel safe and understood. While our inner child wants to be taken care of without having to do anything, if we are to embody our mature adult self, we have to take responsibility for communicating our needs and desires.

OVERCOMING GUILT

Establishing boundaries can mean we have to navigate feelings of guilt. Many of us don't set boundaries to avoid guilt, but ultimately, the longer we wait, the harder it gets. We might avoid hard conversations because we don't want to deal with the backlash of someone's emotional reaction or to avoid our own tough feelings. We might deny our truth or do our best to ignore something that's clearly out of alignment. But this strategy only works for so long because it isn't rooted in truth. When something is keeping us up at night or eating at us all day long, it's time to say something.

It's normal to feel a mix of emotions when you're just finding your way in boundary-setting. You may feel the urge to take your decision back or rush in to make someone else feel better right after you've said no. You don't need to save them. Do your best to breathe through it, and it will get easier.

WHEN A BOUNDARY HAS BEEN CROSSED

When someone has crossed a boundary, we need to communicate and make a request for how we would like them to show up in the future. More serious boundary violations sometimes require outside support or professional help. Sometimes we can't do it all on our own because it's not safe to do so.

There will be times when, even though we love someone, the highest choice is to remove their energy from our life in service to our hearts. In a relationship, just speaking or hearing the words "I love you" does not replace the need for respect, honesty, authenticity, and freedom of expression. We can love others and still put ourselves first. No one else is going to do that for us. It is our job to ensure that we are loving and being loved to our fullest potential. We can love someone and understand "why" they do what they do, and still not allow them to cause us any further heartache.

Understanding the root of someone's pain means we can see that they are operating from a wound and repeating their own trauma. We do not need to demonize them or allow their behavior to define our worth. We must also remember that it is not up to us to rescue people from their pain. We are not responsible for healing their wounds or fixing their troubles and we cannot be a bottomless bucket for another person's trauma. We must protect our energy and honor ourselves.

SEXUAL BOUNDARIES

Something that isn't often spoken about is the impact that sexual trauma can have on our ability to set boundaries and say no in the future.

When our physical boundaries have been violated, there is often a lot of healing to do so that we can reclaim our voice and sovereignty over our body. Never be ashamed if there were moments in your history where you feel you "should" have said no but didn't or couldn't. When our survival feels threatened, our nervous system can respond by freezing or fawning as a form of self-protection. This can look like numbing, shutting down, or working to appease someone even though they are taking advantage of us or aren't a safe person. Recovering from this will require gentleness and understanding. If you have healing to do around your sexuality, you may need to make certain adjustments, go at a slower pace, or have vulnerable conversations about what you need to feel safe as you heal.

When it comes to sexuality and how you express yourself, there is no right or wrong way, but there are things to keep in mind when you're getting to know someone with the intention of building a relationship. Sex is bonding, so it's often wise to wait until we feel clear that we want to go further into a relationship. However, sometimes we set a boundary around sex or physical intimacy with a person and then the moment takes hold. So what do you do if you find yourself in a situation where you've crossed your own boundary?

It's your body, and you're allowed to change your mind. You can have sex once and decide you don't want to have sex again for a while, or ever. You're also free to have casual sex with whomever you choose, because you have a right to experience and own your pleasure! When it comes to sexual boundaries, listening to your body and trusting how you feel are vital. Good sexual boundaries will look unique to each of us based on our personal philosophies, personalities, and preferences, but practicing good self-care and communicating our needs are at the heart of healing our relationship to our body. Most importantly, we need to be radically honest with ourselves and be willing to make adjustments if our feelings change along the way.

THINGS TO CONSIDER BEFORE YOU PHYSICALLY ENGAGE

- Do you feel safe in your body with this person?
- Do you feel respected and heard by this person?
- Are you having sex to receive love, or because you genuinely feel a desire to have sex with this person?
- Do you feel safe to ask for what you need during sex or after?
- Do you want to have sex with this person again?
- Are you energetically sensitive? How will this interaction impact you tomorrow, or a week from now?

IS IT A WALL OR A BOUNDARY?

Walls serve to guard our heart and prevent people from seeing us fully. Boundaries serve to protect us and keep people at a healthy distance. However, secure boundaries also connect us to people and invite them into our lives in a way that feels safe and good.

Only you will know for sure whether you are creating walls or setting boundaries, so your practice is to return to your body any time you're not sure and check in with yourself. Are you feeling scared? Are you shutting down? Is there something you need before you can feel safe in connection again? Do you require some time or space to gain clarity? Get to know yourself. It's okay if sometimes your walls are up; get curious rather than self-critical. Then you can determine whether a change is necessary or whether a fear is being activated and your inner child needs tending.

A WALL LOOKS LIKE

- Empty threats or ultimatums
- Something that holds us back from having intimate relationships
- Harsh or aggressive words or actions
- A lack of flexibility or willingness to collaborate
- A "my way or the highway" mentality

A BOUNDARY LOOKS LIKE

- An invitation for someone to love us better
- A line in the sand around certain types of behaviors we won't accept
- Something we need in order to feel safe in a relationship
- A way of being, relating, or communicating that strengthens a relationship
- Room for collaboration and curiosity

DISCOVERING YOUR AUTHENTIC BOUNDARIES

Our boundaries are personal and can change over time. As you read through these examples, notice what stands out for you. You may realize that some make you feel expansive and resonate with you. Others may feel neutral, while some may cause a contraction. The sensations you feel may point to what some of your boundaries are.

SPIRITUAL BOUNDARIES

- I am open to feedback or spiritual teachings but will choose what feels right for me.
- I don't push my spiritual agenda on others.
- I trust other people to find their own way; it's not my job to save or fix them.

EMOTIONAL BOUNDARIES

- I am not available to hold endless space for others.
- I will respect other people's emotional boundaries by making a request for them to listen before sharing.
- I will communicate when I have the capacity to be there for others and when I don't.
- I am not available to be a mediator between family members.
- I am not responsible for caretaking the feelings of others.
- I ask for help when I need it.

RELATIONSHIP BOUNDARIES

- We speak to each other with kindness.
- We do not yell at each other.
- We agree to talk about our issues within forty-eight hours of conflict.
- We are open and honest with each other.

SELF-CARE BOUNDARIES

- I do not go out past midnight on a work night.
- I do not drink the night before an important meeting.
- I take at least one night to myself per week to journal and to practice self-care.
- I spend one night a week with my friends outside of my romantic partnership.
- I have quiet time to myself every day.

DATING BOUNDARIES

- I meet first dates at places that have an easy exit if things don't feel safe or aligned.
- I ask to meet in a public place for the first time.
- I do not drink on a first date.
- I do not sleep with someone until we've decided we're serious about exploring a committed relationship.
- I am up front that I'm only interested in dating people who are genuinely seeking a committed partnership.
- I communicate if I'm seeking a more casual connection and request the same communication of my dates.
- I do not date people who are actively struggling with an addiction.

Journaling Session: Exploring Your Beliefs about Boundaries

Some of us were taught to be selfless and so we grew to believe that having boundaries is selfish or even mean. To feel empowered in expressing our needs, we must first understand our own beliefs around what boundaries represent. The following journaling questions are designed to help you uncover your unique understanding of boundaries so you can trust yourself and feel confident in expressing your needs.

> *What do you believe boundaries are for?*
>
> *How have you mistaken boundaries for walls in your own life?*
>
> *Can you remember times in your past when you felt guilty for setting a boundary?*
>
> *Do you believe that boundaries make you powerful? If your answer is yes, do you feel safe in your power?*
>
> *Is there any part of you that believes that if you are powerful, you will hurt others?*

You could have all the boundary scripts in the world but if underneath you're operating from a belief that boundaries are mean or selfish, you'll likely never speak up. Sometimes we aren't setting boundaries because we actually fear our own power or anger. We might set rigid boundaries because we are terrified to be taken advantage of or because we have patterns of control to unwind. Know that it's okay to move slowly and take baby steps.

One of the best ways to practice is by setting and keeping small boundaries with yourself. Perhaps you can choose one simple change you'd like to make in your own life. Things like limiting your alcohol intake, saving a little bit of money every month in case of emergency, setting limits with your boss at work, or sticking to a stretching routine may seem minuscule in the grand scheme of things, but when it comes to embodying the kind of person you want to date, this is the place to start. Keeping and honoring the boundaries you set for yourself will grow you into the kind of person you want to be.

THINGS TO REMEMBER

- Boundaries can strengthen relationships.

- Setting new boundaries in relationships that have a long history will require patience. Sometimes the relationship will adjust, and sometimes it will end.

- You have full permission to set, honor, and express your boundaries.

- Your boundaries will shift and change as you grow.

- You may be great at setting boundaries in some relationships and not in others; this may indicate an area that needs your attention.

- When you first start setting boundaries, it may come across as aggressive. Keep trying and practice being in your power in a way that is authentic for you.

- Nobody is perfect. You're never going to get it right 100 percent of the time, and neither will anyone else.

- No one can read your mind. It's your responsibility to clearly and directly communicate your boundaries.

I don't want the honeymoon phase forever.

I want the depth that can only come from having climbed tall mountains and walked the low valleys together.

I don't want the butterflies of excitement and lust; I want the peace of healing and making way for a better future—one influenced by who we inspire each other to be.

I want the kind of love that is calm, devoted, and playful.

Love that does not consume the energy between us like a vacuum but serves as a power grid to redistribute our gifts throughout our community and world.

A love that gives us the energy to serve a higher purpose.

CHAPTER 13

CLARIFY YOUR EXPECTATIONS

WE LIVE IN A TIME OF OPTIONS WHERE THERE ARE dozens of new dating apps every day and where the idea of settling is highly discouraged. But there is a shadow side to a generation of people determined "never to settle," and that is never having *enough*. In our endless pursuit for the perfect relationship, we might lose sight of the reality that no human can meet every single one of our needs and provide us with a constant stream of bliss.

Relationships are a mixed bag. There will be good days and there will be bad days. If we can enter a partnership with a clear sense of who we are and realistic expectations of what a conscious relationship looks like, then we will have the resilience and courage to weather the challenges in an intentional way. We will allow the lessons we learn through our partnerships to become our spiritual teachers.

But what if you don't know whether your expectations are reasonable? Are you really asking for too much, or are you settling for too little? Exactly how do you know when the bar is set too high, too low, or just right? You are unique and what you need to feel nourished in a relationship may be very different from someone else's vision. For this reason, it's not so much about finding concrete lists of what's okay to expect and what's not, but about taking a more philosophical approach that allows us to bring wisdom, and self-awareness into our relationships.

Most of the time the blocks we run into in love are related to fear—fear of being abandoned, of losing love, of not being enough, or of being too much. These fears can manifest in a variety of ways, but most commonly they will present as either settling for poor treatment or having such rigid expectations that no one will ever fit the bill. This chapter is designed to help you see where you're being *self-honoring* by holding healthy expectations, and where you may be overly *self-protecting* by having rigid or unrealistic expectations.

OUR QUEST FOR PERFECTION

As long as we expect a partner to be our everything, meet 100 percent of our needs, always understand us, and never come across as insensitive, we will be forever on the hunt for love. You're not going to find a person out there who is all these things, and it has nothing to do with what you deserve or how much work you've done on yourself. To put it quite bluntly, this person does not exist!

There is no perfect partner. There is no enlightened being who is fully conscious all the time, who will never accidentally hurt your feelings, and who will give you everything you want at every moment of the day. Growth comes in surrendering to this reality—in seeing your partner as human and loving them in all their forms.

The magic happens when we move toward consciousness in union with another. It's found in the bumps along the way, in the stumbling upon each other's baggage and unpacking it, laughing at it, embracing it, dancing with it, and not rejecting it. There are endless ways to guard the heart, to pick another apart, to say they aren't enough, too much of this or too much of that, but underneath lies our own inner fears: *Is it safe to want this much? Is it safe to show all of myself?*

Seeking perfection is a strategy to self-protect, a sneaky way to stay separate from love, to affirm an old story, to avoid exposing our wounds. When we have a realistic and integrated lens of what a healthy relationship looks like and we are at home in our most empowered version of ourselves, we can set boundaries and honor our emotional needs while also allowing our partners to be imperfect. Accepting that love is imperfect does not mean letting go of our standards or the vison of love we want. We are allowed to want what we want out of a relationship.

We all deserve a partner who is emotionally available, committed, honest, and willing to move through tough times. It's not unrealistic to want a partner who is interested in doing the work with you, or someone who aligns with you on a spiritual level. However, even in the most aligned partnership, there will be differences or qualities that challenge the relationship. We have to make room for those differences and learn to appreciate what people bring into our lives *because* they are different from us. And oddly enough, the thing we are most attracted to in the beginning with our partners often will be the thing we struggle with the most later on.

I once worked with a woman in a group session named Nadia. She was powerful, self-expressed, and intensely clear on what she was looking for in a partner. Right away I could sense that Nadia was very comfortable with her fire—leadership, directness, and confidence came easily for her. However, she also complained that while dating, none of her potential suitors asked many questions or pursued her the way she desired. She would just keep asking them questions and sharing about herself, and while these men enjoyed who she was and often showered her in compliments, they weren't taking initiative like she was.

Each person in a relationship tends to favor and embody more of one element—earth, air, fire, or water—than all of the rest. As is often the case, Nadia was drawing in more watery emotional types who had less fire, and therefore were bringing a different energy to her. I suggested that she lean out and make room for them to step more into the energy she was taking up by asking fewer questions and letting the conversations die if they weren't willing to engage.

While Nadia and I explored this further, she expressed her admiration for my partnership with Ben and how much she wanted a relationship like ours. It inspired me to let her into my world a little bit, to show her how my relationship had its own challenges. "What you may not realize is that the thing I am most attracted to in my partner, his fire and leadership, is also what triggers me the most!" I told her.

I always wanted a partner who would plan adventures, take the lead, and contribute equally, and Ben does all of those things so beautifully. I'm very comfortable with my fire and have a strong independent streak, but I am also highly sensitive and crave water and gentleness in my life. And the element he is most challenged with is water! So, of course, our work is in learning to navigate the emotional realms together—for him to soften and let me in, and for me to be patient and kind when he isn't my perfect balance of both elements. The more we relax into acceptance, the more rapidly things seem to shift for the better. Nadia listened intently as I shared and her body posture noticeably relaxed. "I feel so seen and understood," she said. "I think I finally get it." I suggested to Nadia that she work with the elemental altar (chapter 3) to celebrate her fire while carving out an invitation to step into her more watery, sensitive side.

We will always have work to do in a relationship no matter whom we choose, so the question is not "Are they everything I want?" but "Is this the person I'm excited to grow and learn with?"

UNREALISTIC EXPECTATIONS

- There will never be conflict.
- Your partner will meet all of your needs.
- Your partner will always make you feel good.
- You will never hurt each other's feelings.
- Your partner will be available to you whenever you want them to be.
- Your partner will be able to hold space for you when you're lashing out.
- You partner will always have the same agenda as you do.
- You partner will think, act, and be like you.
- Your partner will take away your pain or internal suffering.

REALISTIC EXPECTATIONS

- You will feel safe and respected with your partner.
- Your relationship will be loving, honest, and committed.
- You can experience play, laughter, pleasure, and trust in your relationship.
- Your partner will be open to learning how to be in conflict together in a healthy way.

- Your partnership is rooted in a mutual willingness to grow together.

- Your partnership allows you to feel safe, seen, and respected in conflict.

- Your partner will have common and different interests.

- Your partner will put the relationship first, but will also prioritize friends and family.

- Your relationship will always require that you both put in the work.

EVEN HEALTHY RELATIONSHIPS HAVE CONFLICT

I've had countless people come to me frustrated when their partners have said they believed that in the right relationship there would be no conflict. I used to believe this one myself! But I can guarantee, *all relationships will have conflict!* We fantasize about relationships without conflict when we don't know how to deal with it. We are either afraid of it, avoid it altogether, or don't know how to stay grounded without losing ourselves when an argument arises.

Learning how to be in a disagreement with our partner in a healthy way gives us an incredible opportunity to explore our mind and to be more vulnerable with them. There's a lot of healing that can happen when we view conflict as a window into our own mind. With practice, we can put down our swords and, rather than fight each other to be right, or hurl our projections at each other, we can let our partners in on our emotional reality and even learn something about our history that will help us love each other better.

In a healthy relationship, we go through cycles. Just like the seasons, we will have periods where things feel light and fun (summer) and where things feel more challenging (winter). As we go deeper into relationship, the goal is to learn how to welcome each season and the medicine it brings with it.

GIVING VOICE TO OUR DESIRES

Just like we cannot expect people to read our minds when it comes to knowing our boundaries, we must also practice giving voice to our expectations. Whether it's out on a date or with a long-term partner, there are always moments of being very connected and in tune with each other, and natural moments of being out of sync and missing cues. Relationships are a dance between asking for what we want and need and knowing when to soften and loosen our grip. This is an art that requires patience and a dash of humor. It asks us to recognize when we are holding on too tightly or expecting things to only be a certain way, and as a result, building resentment or missing out on an opportunity to enjoy the connection just as it is.

If you find yourself feeling resentful in your relationships, it's safe to assume that there are unspoken expectations at the helm. Resentment comes as a reminder to be honest with what we desire, acknowledge where we feel like we're not being met, and give voice to what we yearn for.

A girlfriend of mine shared that she had a tendency to develop "imaginationships." Imaginationships are when we craft a relationship with another person in our mind without having direct conversations, leaving a lot of room for misunderstanding and fantasy. At times she was convinced that she was in a relationship with a person and later found out that they were completely unaware! This is the kind of thing that happens when we internalize too much and don't express what we truly want. The best practice for breaking this pattern is to bring your truth forward as early as possible.

SETTING YOUR SIGHTS
ON THE HORIZON

On the other side of unpacking our wounds, moving through the power struggle and ego drama is where the true conscious relationship begins. Where the intensity of the healing work subsides and we begin to embody a deeper spiritual purpose for the relationship. The clearing work is completely necessary, but it is not the destination.

A conscious relationship is a place we arrive once we've taken ownership for the ways our ego tries to keep us safe. It's not that power struggles never happen anymore, or that both partners have attained a high degree of enlightenment and are free of having bad days, but the way it shows up changes considerably when a couple (or each individual) matures and evolves. Little moments of mis-attunement rarely escalate into big or long drawn-out conflicts because there's more mindfulness about use of energy.

So much of our culture is enveloped in the false narrative that "true love" must feel like a tsunami of highs forever. We often interpret the normal transition from new love to mature love as the relationship breaking. The honeymoon phase in many ways can feel like being in a bubble. You carve out extra time for this new person and the focus is on exploration and discovery—it's all very fresh and exciting!

Mature love doesn't mean that you'll no longer feel attracted to your partner or have moments of intensity or deep passion. It means that when you have those experiences, they're more rooted. Mature love is medicinal; it has had time to alchemize the unique ingredients you've each brought to the partnership.

Relationships can be sensually, emotionally, and spiritually energizing long term. In a conscious partnership, a couple might bump into each other's egos, feel annoyed, or have a moment of mis-attunement and simply choose to shake it off and let it go rather than feeding negativity. Set your sights on the horizon and on how beautiful your relationships can be—the healing work does not have to feel hard forever.

Journaling Session: Explore Your Expectations

It's important to explore the expectations you have for your relationships to help you understand recurring patterns that play out in your life. When you recognize which of your expectations are realistic and which are not, you set the foundation for a conscious relationship. Grab your pen and journal and go through the questions below. Be honest with yourself as you answer each prompt and return to chapter 10 any time you need to revisit self-compassion rituals.

What do you notice about your relationship to conflict?

How do you think your relationship should look and be?

What are some of the biggest disappointments you've experienced in your relationships?

When you tune in for a moment, were the disappointments amplified by the belief that things were supposed to happen a specific way, but didn't end up being what you'd expected?

Where did you learn that things were supposed to be a certain way (e.g., watching a lot of romantic comedies; growing up on Disney)?

MOVING FROM EXPECTATIONS TO CORE VALUES

The Latin root of the word expectations is *expectationem*, meaning "an awaiting." Expectations are defined as a strong belief that something will happen or be the case in the future. But relationships don't work that way—they can't be calculated, predicted, or boxed in.

The less we hold on to rigid expectations and allow things to unfold naturally, the happier we will be. If we're always waiting for our partner to say or do something, we're setting ourselves up for disappointment. We may make up fantasy scenarios in our mind and then be let down when reality presents us with something else.

When we go into any situation, dynamic, or relationship without the weight of specific expectations, we find peace. People don't always do things on our time line—say I love you, say thank you, acknowledge you for doing the dishes, notice that you swept the floor or whatever nice thing you did. There are always moments where we can choose to let go and find peace.

Becoming a more whole and conscious being means shifting from the idea of forcing or imposing expectations and, instead, bringing with you the core values that inspire you to go deeper into relationship. The root of the word values is "be strong" or "be well." As long as you are operating from your own core values, you can thrive in every area of your life—at work, at home, and in your most intimate relationships. In the next chapter, we'll explore what your values are and what's guiding your choices at this particular phase of your life.

THINGS TO REMEMBER

- Sometimes our expectations are rigid or unrealistic as a way to self-protect.

- The more confident and empowered you are, the easier it will be to balance your expectations in a healthy way.

- In a healthy partnership, there will still be moments of being in sync and out of sync. It takes maturity to move toward acceptance in these moments.

- You're allowed to want what you want. It's not unrealistic to expect love, safety, trust, respect, and commitment from a partner.

- As you heal and mature, your expectations may shift or soften. You may find it easier to let go when things don't happen exactly as planned.

- No one will ever be able to meet all of your needs and expectations. There's a difference between someone who is committed and human (not always in sync with you) and a person who is obviously not interested in showing up.

Our wound will tell us that we aren't enough.
Our worth will remind us we have always been whole.
Our wound will tell us that rejection means we're broken.
Our worth will show us that rejection is redirection.
Our wound will tell us we have to work to be loved.
Our worth knows that love is our birthright.

CHAPTER 14

DEFINE YOUR CORE VALUES

THE BELIEFS AND GUIDING PRINCIPLES THAT WE LIVE our lives by are our *core values*. They are the qualities that are most important to us, like respect, integrity, honesty, loyalty, and generosity. Core values are a road map of who we are in our *highest expression* and how we want to be met in our relationships.

If you know what you value and stand by it, your boundaries naturally become clear to those around you. This is because knowing your truth makes it much easier to communicate it. Knowing what you value means you know what you need to feel aligned, instead of unconsciously adopting the values of those around you and looking to others to tell you who you are and what you should believe.

When we are feeling stuck in repeating patterns, we are often disconnected from our core values. We might overly focus on others, seek approval, or go into full-blown self-abandonment. And with that goes our ability to attract the types of relationships we long for. It may feel as though we're taking a huge risk by standing behind our core values, but by doing so, we're calling in and curating the kind of environment, people, and situations that match our energy.

MAKING ROOM FOR
THE RIGHT PEOPLE

After my divorce, I refused to self-abandon again. I had settled for relationships that weren't in line with my values for far too long. I was no longer willing to stray from what I desired, and it gave me a sense of power in my relationships. Not power over, *but power in.* I felt that I could be 100 percent true to myself and stand in my worth without fear of being rejected. I was ready to have lonely nights, to be single for many, many years if that's what it took.

One night I decided to write down what a partnership that matched my values would look like. I envisioned the way I wanted to feel with my partner, their qualities, how we'd spend our time together, and what our future would be. I even described the ways we would have conflict (that one didn't always go exactly as planned, by the way). I put it all down on a piece of paper and tucked it in my journal.

One of the most specific things I wrote was that he would not drink alcohol. Drinking carried a lot of weight for me. Growing up, I had seen the impact drinking had on my mother and other people I loved. One of my core values is spiritual, emotional, and physical health—and I wanted a partner who shared that value. When I told a friend of mine, he said, "Don't you think that's a little bit unreasonable? Asking to have a partner who doesn't drink is going to make it hard to find someone, and what if he just wants to go out and have a few drinks with his buddies when he's on a trip?"

"Then I don't want to date him," I replied. "Plain and simple: It's just not for me. I want to be with a partner who doesn't drink."

I kept my list, but then became so focused on my own healing journey that I didn't date anyone for a while. Although I received invitations, I could sense fairly quickly that they were not aligned. Then I met Ben, and something in me said yes right away. After a few hangouts, Ben shared that he had been through rehab when he was fifteen years old and did not drink alcohol. When we first met and in the years that followed, I realized the power of truly standing in my desire. Even though people were telling me it was unreasonable or that it was going to make it harder to find someone, my unwavering commitment to myself ultimately created the space for Ben to enter my life.

I wasn't asking anyone to change; I was just calling in somebody who was in alignment with my philosophy for life. And that is how we want to approach dating and relationships in general. Often, in my course, when I hear people say, "Well, this severely limits my options," my response is, "Great, you're only looking for one person!"

PUTTING UP ROADBLOCKS

We humans are complicated creatures. We will find all sorts of sneaky ways to put up roadblocks when it comes to love. In my case, I said I didn't want a partner who drank, but then I could have also just as easily used Ben's past against him. I could have said, "Well, I don't want someone who's been to rehab." In our desire to be with someone who matches our values, we can sometimes take it too far. We may sometimes, instead, make it impossible for people to live up to our standards.

I'm not suggesting that you date someone struggling with an active addiction, as they won't have the capacity to be in an honest and vulnerable relationship (even if they want to) if they are currently prioritizing their addiction. But in my experience, dating or marrying someone who's gone through the 12 Steps and is in full recovery can be incredibly rewarding because they've done something very difficult and chosen to heal. The same goes for dating divorcees.

Some people get divorced and turn bitter. They choose not to learn from the ending of their relationship and go on to repeat the same mistakes from their past. It's usually easy to tell early on who these folks are, because they have an awful lot of things to say about their exes and not much to share in the realm of personal responsibility or insights gleaned from their marriage breaking down. But when I met Ben, he told me he knew he was going to marry a divorced woman. He recognized that a person who had gone through a divorce would make a great partner because they had already experienced heartache and loss, and usually those people know the value of commitment and putting in the work.

It's okay to be clear on what you want, but leave a little wiggle room for people to surprise you. When we let our core values be the compass, rather than scrutinizing the details or mistakes others have made in the past, it's much easier to trust our choices. For instance, a person may have been unfaithful and that led to a divorce, but then immersed themselves in therapy, uncovered their childhood wounds, and learned a lot about what unconsciously drove them to act that way. It's about valuing a growth mind-set, self-awareness, and personal responsibility.

Sometimes it's the people who have the most baggage that become the most attentive and dedicated partners. They are the ones who know their own darkness, have seen crisis and pain, and have endured loss. And despite this, they choose to heal and grow; they understand that relationships require patience. Don't judge a person for their past. Instead, see whether they have the courage and willingness to grow, to be honest, to show up—to try again.

THE LEGENDARY LOVE LETTER

When we know our values, relationships are no longer about other people choosing us. We're the ones choosing. We shift the frame from wondering, "Do they like or approve of me?" to "Does this feel right for me?" We trust that what we want is valid. Instead of externalizing our energy, we let our inner messenger guide the way.

When Ben and I first started seeing each other I had been in the depths of my own inner healing work for almost a year. About a month into our relationship, I began feeling like I needed more clarity on the direction we were headed. So, I asked him if he would be okay with me writing a letter to get all my thoughts out and then we could meet in person to talk. At this stage in my journey, I was clear that I didn't want to hold anything back. I wanted to be in total expression with him from the start. In a way, I was testing him to see how deep he was willing to go with me. And he was testing me in his own ways as well. That's a healthy thing (if we do it consciously rather than in unconscious ways like starting fights or making people guess what we're feeling).

And so, I wrote him a letter about what I was experiencing so far and how I felt about him.

I shared all the things I was working on. I revealed a situation that had triggered me. I owned that my abandonment wound was my responsibility to heal, and that I didn't expect him to do this work for me.

I then shared ways that he could support me and help me feel safe while working through this.

I told him what I yearned for in partnership, what I wanted to create together, what I was willing to give, and how I was willing to show up.

And then I sent it to him.

I felt so at ease with all of it, but when I shared it with my girlfriends at the time, they said, "Are you serious? It's only been a month. I can't believe you did that!" But I trusted myself, and I had a good read on the energy between us to know the door was open for a move like this. Later when I began facilitating women's groups and when Ben and I were married it became this legendary letter in our community because everyone thought it was so bold. And in a way, it was bold. I really took a risk by being that vulnerable and asking for what I wanted early on. He had no choice but to say yes or no. *And it could have been a no.*

When he received the letter, he invited me over to discuss it. He had written a response to each thing I had shared. We laid in bed together in a candlelit room as he read his responses out loud, pausing to look me in the eyes. I remember thinking, "This guy is amazing." He told me what he wanted to give to the relationship and all the experiences that he wanted to have together. It was a really beautiful moment for me to see that this relationship was in line with my values for open-hearted communication, honesty, and respect. I looked him in the eyes and said, "You know, I've been really hurt in the past. I've gone through a divorce. I don't have time to waste, and I also totally honor where you're at. So if you don't want to build a conscious relationship with me, I'm okay to hear your no."

In our case, his answer was yes. But the key was that I was willing to stand in my power and give him the space and freedom to say no, and to love him in that. It worked out for us because we were aligned. Sometimes it won't turn out that way, but the only way to clear a path for what is right for you is to be meticulous with your intentions. Hearing no can also propel you toward the life you want, even if it doesn't feel that way in the moment.

RECLAIMING YOUR CORE VALUES

Reclaiming your core values is about assessing what beliefs or behaviors you adopted based on your family programming and learning to set aside what doesn't belong to you so you can claim what is yours.

Some of the values we inherit from our parents and culture are incredibly valuable. They provide us with a rich sense of identity and belonging. But many of us operate on autopilot, unknowingly living by the values we inherited and never taking stock of whether or not our choices reflect who we really are. Through individuating from our parents, we can step into our wholeness and prioritize the values that help us feel alive, true to ourselves, and connected to the kind of life we want to live.

As levels of consciousness rise, values such as self-preservation, obedience, control, toughness, and status that have been the priority of generations before us are coming out of the shadows and up for review. Many of our ancestors inherited the values of colonialism, which prioritizes individualism, hierarchy, and capitalism rather than community, transparency, and equality. Doing the work to reclaim our core values is also a reclamation of our humanity. It is knowing that each of us is a valuable human being, not because of what we do, but because of who we are.

TAKING INVENTORY OF YOUR PAST

Looking back, the core values that drove me to stay in an abusive relationship when I was nineteen years old were sexual expression and play. This man was very playful, and we had strong physical chemistry. But we didn't have authenticity. We didn't have honesty, accountability, or respect. We also didn't have empathy, emotional intimacy, and deep commitment to ourselves and to inner growth—the very things I value now in my life. I came to realize that choosing a partner based on fun and great sex in the absence of all other values was not enough for a fulfilling relationship.

Our core values can shift and change as we shift and change. We may need to assess which of our values has swung out of empowered expression into shadow expression. Generosity, for instance, can become over-giving and caretaking in its shadow expression. Loyalty is a wonderful quality, though its shadow can become corrosive and lead to martyrdom and putting up with unacceptable behavior for far too long. Exploring our past experiences can help us understand what drove us or attracted us to others in our previous relationships. It can also reveal which beliefs we adopted from our families or caregivers that need to be reevaluated. Most of the world never takes the time to consider what their values are before entering a relationship, so if this is your first time, you're still ahead of the curve. Looking back and taking an inventory of your past values is a compassionate inquiry of where you were in the past, so that you can move forward and reclaim what's true for you now.

Journaling Session: Defining Your Core Values

A core value(s) I inherited from my parent(s) that is true for me is _____.

A core value(s) I have been loyal to from my family conditioning that isn't true to me is _____.

A core value(s) I have been denying to stay loyal to my family conditioning is _____.

Which core values do I tend to prioritize in a relationship?

Which core values do I tend to neglect?

In choosing past partners, my choices show me that I valued _____.

How did these choices impact me and my relationships?

Which core values continue to be important to me?

Which core values am I not willing to compromise going forward?

WHAT MATTERS TO ME NOW

Because there are many outside influences that have the ability to shape our values, it is important to regularly check in with yourself to remember what matters to you throughout various stages of your life. In chapter 16, I'm going to help you create your own "love map," which is similar to a vision board for how you want to show up in your life and what you'd like to create in a future relationship. Knowing the core values you want to prioritize will be a part of this process.

There are many core values that are not on the following list, but you will find extensive versions online with a quick search. The list is meant to activate something within you to propel further self-discovery. As you read the list, I invite you to notice what lights you up. What feels resonant for you? Highlight or write down any of the words that jump out at you. This list is just a starting point. As you continue the path of *Becoming the One*, you will discover more of your core values and what qualities you want to step into yourself.

Abundance	Challenge	Fun
Acceptance	Change	Generosity
Accountability	Choice	Gifts
Acknowledgment	Cleanliness	Gratitude
Adventure	Closeness	Growth
Affection	Collaboration	Harmony
Appreciation	Commitment	Health
Authenticity	Community	Honesty
Autonomy	Companionship	Hope
Awareness	Contribution	Humility
Balance	Creativity	Humor
Beauty	Family	Inclusion
Belonging	Freedom	Independence
Candor	Friendship	Innovation

Inspiration	Recognition	Self-acceptance
Integrity	Reliability	Self-awareness
Optimism	Religion and Faith	Self-expression
Presence	Respect	Self-respect
Punctuality	Risk-taking	Sensitivity
Purpose	Safety	Sensuality
Quality Time	Security	Spirituality

EMBODYING YOUR CORE VALUES

Living in alignment with our values means embodying the qualities we care about most. We are quick to look outside of ourselves and make demands of others, but this work will require you to go within and evaluate where you may be straying from your truth.

One of the most common ways this shows up is in our relationship to commitment. If we deeply desire commitment from others, first we must take an honest look at our own relationship to commitment. Any quality we crave in others is also waiting to come alive in us. Embodying our values means getting to the point where you no longer only say, "I desire these qualities" but "I am these qualities."

When we practice this, we become magnetic. We draw people into our field who complement our lives and share similar values. More than that, we can experience true inner freedom and contentment because the world we've created for ourselves reflects who we are at our core.

Embodying our values is a daily practice. If you appreciate compassionate communication, how can you practice embodying that with others? If you value commitment, where in your life can you honor your commitments more? If you value play and adventure, where can you invite more of this in? *Becoming the One* is not about doing it alone. It is about learning how to treat the relationship you have to yourself as an ever unfolding path of magic, truth, and devotion.

THINGS TO REMEMBER

- Core values are a road map of who you are in your *highest expression*—the most self-honoring and authentic part of your being.

- Core values can bring you closer to what you want, and help weed out the situations, people, and environments that you don't want.

- Claiming your core values requires courage! Some people will not be able to meet you where you're at, and that's okay.

- Beneath the fear of claiming your core values is a fear that you're not worthy or good enough. Bring nurturance and love to your fear and remember that you are worthy and capable of creating the type of relationship your heart desires!

- Your body can help guide you toward what is right for you and what isn't.

PART FIVE

GET WHAT
YOU WANT
IN YOUR
RELATIONSHIP

Maturing in relationship means recognizing
that there will always be things to work on.
It's learning to ride the ebbs and flows that
partnership can bring, without expecting
perfection from our partners or ourselves.

CHAPTER 15

CREATING A CONSCIOUS RELATIONSHIP

RELATIONSHIPS ARE A COSMICALLY DESIGNED CON-tainer for spiritual evolution. No matter which direction they take us, we can always come away with a lesson. They highlight our patterns, sometimes not so gently awakening the parts of us that were once asleep. When entered with intention and willingness, they can initiate potent healing for every person with the courage to sit in the fire of transformation.

Healing is not only an inside job; it is also a cocreative process that requires us to dance in connection and play with our hearts wide open. Do not wait to let love in until you have it all figured out; that day will never come. Do not wait until you are certain you have arrived; you may die and rebirth a thousand times in this one life. Healing is forever unfolding; life is happening now. The intention behind deepening your relationship to *you*, to *Becoming the One*, is not to eradicate your need for connection or the desire to find a partner, but to find your rightful resting place—at home in your own body, heart, and soul.

True transformation happens when our body feels safe enough to finally release held emotional memory. For this shift to occur, we require the warm presence of others with healthy and securely attached nervous systems. Individualistic healing work and spiritual teachings are on the mark when it comes to recognizing that we must heal ourselves to heal the world, but it cannot be done without the healing power of relationship—friendship, community, and romantic partnership alike. Relationship matters.

Unlocking the patterns that hold us back is about tending to the wound that chooses a familiar pain over unknown happiness and bliss. Throughout this book, we've uncovered what dictates our patterns and creates pain in our lives, and now it's time to embrace the beauty that relationship can bring and set a new precedent for how we will relate to others moving forward. This chapter is devoted to creating a new lens for how to see relationships and their purpose in our lives.

AM I READY TO BE IN A RELATIONSHIP?

When we enter a relationship with another person, in a sense we are taking on their soul work too. For this reason, there are times when it is very wise to embark on the healing journey solo and take some time to yourself before entering a relationship. When we're in a self-loathing place or feeling desperate for connection, we're more likely to settle for scraps, or as I like to call it, "Dumpster diving for love." We want to choose partnerships from a clear and grounded place, but our patterns don't vanish— they just shape-shift—and it's often when we meet someone who we can go all the way with that a whole new flavor to the work is born.

When I work with folks in my programs, they often worry that they haven't done enough of the inner work to be ready for a relationship, or they fear that they need to be completely finished healing before they meet someone. *In this work, no one is ever finished.*

We might feel like we've finally healed our wounds and figured things out, only to have it all flood back to us once we enter a partnership. We cannot clear everything on our own; there will always be more to explore when we couple up. If you're not sure whether you're ready, rather than trying to self-assess how "healed" you are (this is a trap), instead ask yourself: "Am I in a place where I have the strength to say no to what doesn't align?" and "Can I be happy on my own, not seeking to fill a void?" If the answer to both is yes, you're ready. If the answer is no, consider spending a bit more time on self-nurturing behaviors so that you can confidently claim what you want.

TWO TYPES OF RELATIONSHIPS: VACUUM AND POWER GRID

Many of us have grown accustomed to simply falling into relationships, rather than entering with intention and a dedication to learning more about ourselves in the process. Redefining what relationship means to you can lay the foundation for your love map, the next and final ritual in this book. To unlearn the old model of relationship and embody a more empowered version, we must know the difference between a vacuum relationship (conventional, nongrowth oriented) and a power-grid relationship (conscious, growth oriented).

What makes a relationship *conscious?* First, each partner must have a clean relationship with themselves. This begins with learning to observe your mind and be a witness to your thoughts, rather than reacting to every thought you have. No one is conscious 100 percent of the time in their relationships, but those who experience the most ease and joy are also the ones who have a high degree of personal responsibility for their own emotions and behaviors; they trust themselves enough to know that sometimes they are wrong, projecting, or simply having an off day. We must also have a bridge between our head and our heart, so that we can challenge our minds, learn when to slow down, and trust our body wisdom.

Vacuum relationships are in many ways there to solve feelings of loneliness or discomfort, a craving for something that's missing. *Power-grid relationships*, or conscious relationships, are an entity of their own: They nourish us on a soul level in ways that conventional relationships simply cannot.

When it comes to tending and contributing to the energy of our relationships, we must be anchored in reciprocity.

In a vacuum relationship, all the energy is sucked dry in our pursuit of fulfilling the need for validation and love. Ultimately, this type of dynamic makes us feel good in the moment, but when that doesn't last, we may blame our partners, find ourselves back in another power struggle, or wonder where we went wrong. When one or both people are constantly focused on taking energy, eventually there is nothing left to give, and we move from one partner to the next, in an endless pursuit of finding "The One" who will solve our problems and make our pain go away.

In a power-grid relationship, the partnership becomes a source of reciprocal energy that fuels our purpose and empowers us to be of service in the world and in our communities. Power-grid relationships help us grow spiritually and emotionally, and that will not always be easy. It will require that we traverse the depths of our own awareness to release old ideas about how relationships "should" look.

VACUUM RELATIONSHIP MENTALITY	POWER-GRID RELATIONSHIP MENTALITY
My partner is the answer to all my problems; they can take my pain away.	I bring awareness to my problems and work on them without needing my partner to fix them for me.
When I find "The One," my past relationship patterns will naturally go away.	When I find "The One," I will still have to work on my patterns.
I'm not whole without a partner.	I am whole and complete as I am.
My partner should meet all of my needs.	It's unrealistic to think my partner can meet all of my needs.
In conflict, someone is right and someone is wrong.	Conflict is an opportunity to learn about myself and my partner.
I have nothing to do with my relationship unhappiness.	I am responsible for my happiness.
My partner should know what I want and need without me having to tell them.	I am responsible for telling my partner what I need and asking for what I want.
When my partner misunderstands me, it means they don't care or I am hard to love.	My partner's words and actions do not define me or my worth.
Secret keeping isn't lying; it's just not telling them everything.	Transparency is key. I let my partner into my world.
Going to therapy means there's something wrong with us.	It's okay to ask for help and seek support.
I listen to respond.	I listen to understand.

THE STAGES OF RELATIONSHIP

Relationships of all kinds go through stages, though our romantic relationships are where the stages tend to be amplified in intensity because they are the ones with the highest stakes.

As I take you through each of these stages, you may see your past or present relationships in many or all of them. The power struggle in particular is the place in which most of our relationships reside, until we hit the same wall one too many times and throw in the towel only to continue our search for "The One." Or we exhaust ourselves with our patterns, roll up our sleeves, and get to work so that we can break the cycle, become our own source of energy, and step into a new way of doing relationship altogether.

Every couple will go through nearly all these stages many times in their relationship cycle. We are all programmed to want the honeymoon phase (spring season) of a relationship. We relish in the newness, budding with fresh energy, passion, and mystery. We aren't taught that long-term relationships have phases and cycles just like every other living being on the planet. So when fall and winter hit, we often feel defeated, lost, and confused. Where did the love go? Why is the passion gone? I guess we've just fallen out of love. But one of the vital errors we make is assuming the relationship is over when the seasons shift rather than embracing change and letting go of what needs to die to make space to birth new energy in the relationship.

Relationships are meant to shift, change, shed, and renew. We need to accept that fall and winter will eventually come and that we need to gather the resources and communication tools to make it through when they do. With the right mind-set, journeying through the cycles of partnership can be even more rewarding than the initial highs we experience in the beginning. Below are the phases that virtually every human being who enters partnership will experience in some shape or form, except for the no relationship zone, which is more of a pattern than a fixed stage of relationship.

The honeymoon phase, power struggle, twilight zone, and conscious relationship are not linear or fixed. We may experience only one or all of these stages in a relationship, or we may move in and out of different stages as we grow and encounter new challenges with a partner. Ultimately, we want to land in conscious relationship territory, which is what *Becoming the One* has prepared you for.

No Relationship Zone

The no relationship zone is part of a common relationship pattern, but unlike the other stages, not everyone will experience this zone. Women I've worked with who report being in this stage find they can never get far enough to enter a relationship. This can look like being in the "friend zone," dating a lot but never finding anyone who turns them on or sparks intimate connection, meeting people who seem like a match but quickly finding out there's a fundamental incongruence, or encountering major red flags. It can also present as struggling to feel anything at all when dating. Having little interest in others and always finding something "wrong" with the person is a commonly shared experience among those who find themselves looping in the no relationship zone. Ending this cycle often requires a renewed willingness to come back to the body and redirect focus toward feeling safe so the heart can soften and authentically open.

Honeymoon Phase

The honeymoon phase can be a wonderful and exhilarating time. We're getting to know a person for the first time, and we often give and receive more energy, attention, and praise while the oxytocin is flowing freely. And while the honeymoon phase is certainly fun to be in, it has some caution signs posted along the way.

In the honeymoon phase, we often begin by idealizing our partner. Nothing they say or do seems to bother us. We may be so caught up in the excitement of getting to know this new person that we ignore red flags, miss little (or not so little) incongruences, or disregard our internal guidance system in service to the chemistry we feel. Eventually, when we begin to get closer to another person, our egos may react to our core wounds and we begin to pick apart the other person, act out, or fall back into our old coping mechanisms, like anxiously chasing, avoiding, or instigating conflict. The honeymoon phase is the most passionate and "romantic" phase, though it's often a more ungrounded experience, where much of our fantasy is projected and imagination is at the wheel. Throughout this book you have learned different tools and practices to stay connected to your body, observe your mind, and remain clear even when the energy is high. It's not that you can't enjoy this phase, but you can do so while also taking good care of yourself first and remaining true to your values.

Power Struggle

In this phase, we begin to move deeper into a relationship with a person. This is when the happy chemicals begin to taper down and our day-to-day reality begins to set in. Now that we're not as ruled by our hormonal or physical urges, we might begin to see this person differently than we initially saw them. In this process, our egos can flair and often our deepest wounds can be activated by the fear of closeness.

Almost all people have some form of self-esteem work to do, and certain individuals with deeper childhood trauma, loss of a parent, or abandonment wounds will often have a belief that on some level they are broken or unworthy of receiving love. The ego's reaction to these fears can be to push love away unconsciously. In the power struggle phase, the partners may be reacting from their wounds and their fears rather than being in their hearts with one another. To get out of this phase, both people have to commit to the inner work and take personal responsibility for their healing.

The Twilight Zone

In the twilight zone, the relationship is starting to flatline. This happens when we stay together but stop putting in the effort. At this stage, we might feel bored, complacent, or full of resentment. Couples either break up or settle into mediocrity with each other until something shakes things up—this can be an affair, a spiritual awakening, a crisis, or one person simply having enough. Harville Hendrix and Helen LaKelly Hunt refer to this stage as "parallel" and my past teacher P. T. Mistbleberger referred to it as "the dead zone."

Though it is common for long-term relationships to have their moments of disconnection, not everyone has to enter the twilight zone if they practice being open with each other and tending to the relationship. For those who find themselves here, it takes a desire to shift the energy on both sides to evolve a relationship past this stage. Most couples in this stage need to prioritize play and fun to infuse life back into their partnership. They also need to clear past resentments and commit to radical honesty so that energy can flow freely between them again. If a couple successfully does this, they can transcend the twilight zone and create a conscious relationship.

Conscious Relationship: The Power Grid

When we enter conscious relationship, our partnership is also a mutually reciprocated friendship, with two people who generate their own energy and share a commitment to truth and soul evolution. As we move into this stage, there is a maturity that has occurred between partners. No longer is the relationship a source of validation or approval, but a complement to an already function-ing, whole, and discerning human being. In conscious relationship, the partnership isn't a crutch or a place to hide; it is illuminating and expansive, a space to grow and thrive.

Journaling Session: Looking Back

Reflect back on the exercises in chapter 9, "Transform Your Relationship Patterns," and relate your findings to the stages of relationship. Which stages of relationship do you recog-nize most in your past relationships? Have you ever had experiences of being in a conscious relationship? If yes, what were you and your partner doing differently?

BE THE KIND OF PERSON
YOU'D WANT TO DATE

I used to work with a mentor who had this question written on the giant whiteboard at the front of his class: "Would you date you?" Often followed by giggles and gasps, we would all shift in our seats at the thought of whether we would truly want to date ourselves. This is where compassionate self-awareness and ownership work fit in.

When we are radically honest with ourselves, we may see that some of the ways we show up in relationship are not in service to our highest good. The Latin origin of the word *radical* is *root*. This reminds us that true honesty must go beyond external blame to the core of our own experience. To be radically honest, we must also be radically accountable. Being aware of our inner saboteur that gets in the way takes courage and maturity, and it gives us the clarity we need to become a more secure version of ourselves.

Of course, you wouldn't actually want to date a person who is exactly like you. It would be boring and there would likely be very little learning for either you. That is why we attract partners and friends who embody qualities that complement or are opposite to us. They invite us to experience a way of being in the world that is slightly different (or completely different) from how we'd naturally do things on our own. This is good! It gives us space to expand, learn, and grow.

However, being the kind of person you want to date is not that literal. This is about energy and embodiment.

We all know what it's like to be around a person who is constantly miserable, closed to life, and negative or judgmental in their patterns and habits. Some of us grew up with family members who slowly hurt themselves by making poor lifestyle decisions or neglecting their own self-care, and we felt the impact of that. We also know what it's like to be around a person who is committed to being awake and of service in the world, someone who genuinely cares for others and understands their worth. We know the difference between a closed heart and an open, tender one. Be the kind of person you would want to date by embodying the qualities you seek in others.

HOW TO PRACTICE CONSCIOUS DATING

Conscious dating is about bringing presence, honesty, and an open mind with you into any new interaction. It is a way of slowing down long enough to get to know each other more deeply and *qualify* each other before diving into a partnership. For an ocean type who identifies as anxious at times, this can be unnerving. We rush into relationships to secure commitment when we want to get rid of our anxiety. For a wind type or person with avoidant tendencies, this will be scary in a different way—because it will require that we lean into connection rather than seek comfort in separateness. You may also find that as you integrate one of these practices, you naturally begin to present as a new elemental type and have a whole new lesson to work on. Celebrate this if and when it happens.

CONSCIOUS DATING IS

- Being authentic
- Listening to your body
- Accepting that being true to yourself will likely mean hearing "no" more often
- Taking time to get to know someone on a deep level
- Asking important questions and being curious about the other person
- Going on dates that reflect your personality and who you are
- Seeing what it feels like to just "be" with this person—go for a walk, have tea, or sit and talk together
- Practicing your boundaries

QUALIFYING THE RELATIONSHIP: QUESTIONS TO ASK YOURSELF

- Do I like how this person speaks to me and others?
- Do I know who this person is, what their past is, and what their core values are when it comes to love and intimacy?
- Is this a person I feel like I could be close friends with or is it just a sexual attraction?
- Do I want something from this person that might be coming from an unconscious place?

- Do I feel like I want them to tell me I'm good enough, confirm that I'm worthy, or validate me in some way?
- Do I feel relaxed, in my body, and safe to express myself with this person?
- Can I have fun, laugh, and be playful with this person? Does the connection feel expansive?

Falling in Love

We first meet.

Our eyes lock, hearts race, and endorphins flow.

From a distance, you are everything I've always wanted but could never quite find.

Maybe you are The One?

Perhaps you are the person with whom all of my patterns and walls will melt away.

Perhaps you are my mother's absent love and my father's devotional presence.

In my eyes, you are God.

I see perfection. I see whatever I want to see.

But wait, as you come closer . . . there is more.

What is it that I feel; old fears and familiar patterns creeping back up?

Who is this?

The "me behind the mask" that I though had vanished, as I put on my best face, and we both basked in the glow of new love.

And who are you, if not the person I hoped you would be?

No matter where we go, our patterns will follow.

No matter who we meet, we cannot outrun our own healing work.

Don't rush; mature love takes time.

The wound may seek security and find false safety in moving quickly, but mindfulness in love asks for patience.

Move not only from the head or the heart, but together in unison.

Give from a place of self-love, and always reserve some for you.

If giving will bring resentment or lack, keep it for yourself.

Only give away what feels abundant in you.

Mature love does not require performance.

Let new love be a dance of exploration, discovery, and possibility.

*Be willing to release it, too,
because sometimes that is the best thing,
and no one has to be made wrong for this.*

You are whole and complete on your own.

Be your own lover first.

Love is all around you.

TENDING TO YOUR RELATIONSHIPS

When you first plant a seed, you need to water it daily. At first, the seed needs more of your attention and nurturance to sprout. Without it, the seed may never sprout at all. As the seedling begins to sprout and grow stronger, you can get away with watering it a bit less, but you still need to weed around it, give it water, and eventually it will bear you food. Nourishment comes directly from the amount of energy you put in to ensure the plant can grow healthy, vital, and nutrient rich—and there are also environmental factors like sunlight, soil quality, and weather patterns. If you neglect the plant for long enough, or if it's in an environment that doesn't support its growth, it will die and stop producing. This is how most things we grow work, and that also goes for our relationships.

We need to tend to our relationships for them to continue to nourish us. Keep in mind that when you sow a garden, there will be some seeds that never sprout at all—and this is how life goes. Not every relationship in your life is meant to go all the way; some nonstarters or endings are to be expected and embraced. Each person who enters your life has a teaching for you and it doesn't matter how long or short the relationship is—this is the practice of conscious relationship.

The cultural story is that relationships are something we go out and find. Our partners are there to make us feel good, to make us whole. But rarely do we see a relationship for what it is: something sacred that carries an energy and frequency of its own. Tending to our relationships is easy in the beginning, but when we get comfortable, we might forget to continue putting in energy. And that's where the relationship becomes stagnant, we lose chemistry, the power struggle permeates the entire relationship, or we start to wonder whether the love is gone. *The truth is, if you want your relationships to continually give you energy, you have to give energy to your relationships.*

A CONSCIOUS PARTNERSHIP IS

- A daily recommitment to show up with an open heart
- Being committed to self-awareness and personal responsibility
- Being engaged in healing wounds from the past
- Making mistakes and saying the wrong thing sometimes
- Reacting from an old wound and practicing compassion
- Recognizing when we project our fears and judgments
- Being willing to apologize
- Learning how to show up more self-aware in conflict
- Practicing acceptance and forgiveness

THINGS TO REMEMBER

- A vacuum relationship is all take and no give, where we see the other as our source of energy and validation.

- A power-grid relationship is built on reciprocity and anchors you in purpose, service, and love.

- Friendships and community connections are also places we can practice conscious relating, not just in a romantic context.

- A conscious relationship requires a constant commitment to honesty, personal responsibility, and inner awareness.

- All relationships have cycles and seasons. We can learn a lot in the darker times and come out stronger.

- *Becoming the One* is about owning your power, embodying radiance, and honoring your truth.

Be brave enough . . .
To leave when it's time
To say I'm sorry
To say I love you
To let go
To love again.

Be brave enough . . .
To be alone
To trust yourself
To listen to that little voice
You know the one
It's not going anywhere.

Be brave enough
To honor your life as your own
To claim your power
And own your fear.

Please don't wait for the dust to settle
And resign to "the way it is"
If you want more . . .
Wake up and claim it!
Wild one, find your wings.

For your kin and every other person who truly cannot
For the sake of your life
Your fire, and all that you can be,
Be brave enough
To Rise.

CHAPTER 16

YOUR PATH TO AUTHENTIC LOVE

IF YOUR DREAM IS TO LIVE IN NATURE IN A HUMBLE home, grow food, have a family, and lead a quiet life, you are enough. If your dream is to travel and live unconventionally, you are enough. If you are a spiritual seeker and you wish to study and dive into the depths of what the realms in between have to offer, you are enough.

When we choose to live in alignment with our dreams and values, we come to understand our worth deep within our soul. A person who claims their voice is unstoppable and inspirational, because in our society what's more common is to sweep our desires under the rug, put ourselves last, and settle for what we are given. You're not one of those people.

Contrary to what we see in the media, being confident in ourselves and our dreams doesn't have to be loud or in your face. There is also a quiet confidence, an inner knowing that you are worthy of having the life you want, a knowing so deep and connected to Spirit that you do not require anyone's approval or permission.

The beautiful thing is that coming into this powerful relationship with ourselves invites others to do the same. As we no longer live and breathe by the judgments and expectations of others, we are clearing the path in our daily lives and relationships to become a reflection of our authentic selves, rather than our wounds. Our lives become a reflection of our own inner work.

CREATING YOUR
CONSCIOUS LOVE MAP

Rose was a sixty-seven-year-young psychotherapist who enrolled in my *Becoming the One* program. After being divorced for nearly twenty years, she met a man who showered her with gifts, planned everything, and made her feel taken care of.

Five months in, she was devasted when out of nowhere he ghosted her. She picked up the pieces of her broken heart and put them back together while she did the program. "I had done inner child work before," she said, "but I had never really had a dialogue with little me in this way until now. I was surprised that what the little girl in me wanted most was her dad." It was through these inner dialogues that Rose realized that what made that five-month relationship so exhilarating for her was the feeling of being provided for, like a father might have.

"I started planning dates for me and my inner child and really listening to her," Rose said. "I took her shopping once and said, 'I am letting you pick out our new sandals,' which of course had sparkles on them!" She smiled and tucked her long silver hair behind her ears as she shared with the group, "I finally see that this wounded part of me needed to be seen and kept safe by me, not by a man." Rose also made colored pencil drawings of her inner child and a drawing of her conscious love map—an illustrated map of her expectations, core values, and desires for a future relationship. These became visual reminders to be gentle and loving with herself and to stay true to her desires.

Shortly after her love map was complete, she met a wonderful man named Stan. "We talked about the need for safety and honoring our inner children," she said. They talked for hours on an intimate level and on their second date, Stan shared that he felt scared because he had feelings for Rose. She mirrored back to him that she also felt scared but that she really cared for him. "Later that night, I told him about how I was ghosted in my last relationship and asked him to please tell me directly if he wasn't ready for a relationship." Two days later, Stan called her and said he wanted to end the relationship because he wasn't ready. After thirty years of marriage, he'd only been single for two years and he needed more time.

"He had so many of the qualities on my love map," said Rose. "He is an honest man who values personal growth and safety. He kept his word, and I was strong enough to ask for what I wanted and needed. At the end of the goodbye call, I thanked him for all I had learned. Stan gave me an opportunity to practice healthy relating. Although brief, I experienced the first conscious relationship (romantically) of my sixty-seven-year lifetime and now I know that I'm ready for the real thing," she said as her green eyes welled with happy tears.

"I use my conscious love map to guide me in my minute-to-minute decisions during and between dates. I use the map to stay crystal clear about what I want and need in my love relationships. Like any road less traveled, having a map to follow makes the journey easier!"

Rose's story is a brilliant illustration of what happens when we are devoted to our relationship to self. She shows us that it's never too late to open our hearts, and that even if a relationship doesn't last forever, we can still glean insight and remain open for the future.

One of the biggest takeaways I hear from the people I work with is how the process of love mapping helped them stand firmly in their boundaries and end the cycle of settling in their partnerships. It served as a compass, guiding them to choose love from their worth, not their wound.

Now it's time for you to create your own conscious love map. This is a creative process designed to connect you to your heart, your essence, and what you truly want. Let this reflect the journey you've been on throughout this book. A love map is meant to be a physical reminder of the intentions you've set for your life and your future relationships.

STEP 1: ENVISION THE LOVE YOU WANT

Choose a time when you're feeling calm and grounded to go through the journaling questions that follow. Light a candle, make yourself some tea, turn on some music, and let it flow. If you aren't sure about the answer to something, give yourself time and reflect on the core values you discovered in chapter 14.

- What is your vison of a fulfilling relationship? What would give you feelings of contentment, ease, connection, and intimacy?

- If you weren't afraid to truly claim what you desire in love, what would you wish for? (Don't hold back; imagine that you can have exactly what you want.)

- What kind of person do you want to attract as a partner? (Describe as many traits that come to mind without limitation.)

- Who do you want to show up as in your relationship? How do you want to feel, how do you want to act, how does your partner experience you?

- What are you willing to do to cocreate a healthy and fulfilling relationship? What ways will you contribute to a conscious relationship?

- How are you committed to showing up when times get tough, when conflicts arise, or when old wounds get triggered? (Really consider how you'll navigate conflict, what steps you'll take, and how you'll support yourself and your relationship through the trials of life.)

- How do you want to love? What does loving someone look and feel like for you?

- How do you want to assert your boundaries? (Describe in detail how and when you will communicate your boundaries.)

- Will you be led by love or by fear? What does being led by love look like, and what does being led by fear look like?

- If the partner of your dreams showed up in front of you, how would you know? (Try closing your eyes and imagining this. What sensations are in your body?)

When you finish writing, read your answers back to yourself. Get comfortable owning that you know who you are and what you want.

STEP 2: DAY-IN-THE-LIFE JOURNALING

This step is all about writing out what you want your dream relationship and life to look like. Step 1 has prepared you for this. Write in the present moment, as if you were already living it and have everything you want now. Be imaginative and detailed; describe your future as if it's a story. What would a day in this future life look and feel like? This letter can be folded up and kept somewhere safe for your eyes only, or be placed on your altar.

STEP 3: MAKE YOUR VISUAL LOVE MAP

With all that you have uncovered in this process, you are ready to create a visual of your heart's truest desires. As you go through this final step, make it a ritual—something your whole body can participate in, not just your mind. I've seen so many creative love maps from people all over the world. You get to make yours however you would like it to look! To see a gallery of completed love maps, visit SheleanaAiyana.com.

Your love map is about more than your dream relationship; it also represents your relationship to yourself and the world around you. Some folks choose to make a map that is primarily focused on romantic partnership, and that is perfectly fine to do. However, if you want to choose a different theme, you're welcome to do that as well. This process is meant to move you out of your logic-focused brain and into the emotional and imaginative side. You can frame your love map like many members of my programs have and put it up in your room, hang it on the fridge, or place it on your altar.

Love mapping is a process I designed when I went through my divorce all those years ago. I used this exact process to prepare for my partnership with Ben. Your love map is there for you as inspiration and encouragement as you carve out a new way of being in the world.

As you create your conscious love map, refer to steps 1 and 2, and everything you've learned along the way. Consider:

- How you want to show up
- How you want a partner to show up
- What core values you have uncovered
- What you desire most in relationship
- The energy you want to give and receive
- The overall theme you want to bring to life

Examples of Love Maps

Stephanie's Love Map

Bronwen's Love Map

YOU ARE THE ONE

I am so honored that you have made this journey to *Becoming the One*. I hope you celebrate yourself for your devotion to the inner work and for everything that you have discovered, healed, or transformed along the way. I am endlessly inspired by each and every person who commits to breaking painful patterns and living from their hearts.

The work you do to heal your heart has an impact on everything and everyone around you. Now more than ever, it is time for us all to connect to what truly matters so that we can create a safer, more compassionate, and more loving world for future generations.

As you know by now, from time to time you may still draw in people who aren't in alignment spiritually, emotionally, or otherwise, but with the tools you take with you from this book, it's now in your power to draw a line in the sand and choose yourself in those moments.

As you continue to return to the somatic practices and visualizations in this book, you will find that you feel more and more at home in yourself. We never know what life has in store for us, but one thing is for certain: Life is not happening in the waiting room. It's happening right now in this very moment.

CELEBRATING YOUR PATH

Life is a cocreation between you and Spirit. Your life path is not entirely yours to dictate. In Western society and many places around the world, one type of relationship is valued above the rest—committed, monogamous marriage that lasts forever. However, this is only one way to experience romantic relationship and not everyone is destined to live out this exact template.

There are so many ways energy can be expressed through us. As you move forward in the world, make space for the mystery. Your path doesn't have be marriage and family to be a valid spiritual path. Not everyone is here to experience the traditional model of relationship in this life. Some of us are here to learn through marriage; some of us will grow through becoming parents; some of us are here to learn through a non-traditional relationship; some will be Tantric practitioners or be single and practice conscious relating through friendship. Some of us will choose to embrace all these unique paths at different stages of our lives. If you find that a romantic partnership isn't showing up in your life despite your desire, you may be tempted to think something is wrong or that you need to do more work. Be mindful not to impose limits on yourself, as all life paths are valid.

All we can do is lean into love in all her forms—through nature, friendship, and connection to community. And if you do find yourself in a partnership, let the remembrance that you are The One be the energy that guides you.

ACKNOWLEDGMENTS

IMMENSE GRATITUDE AND LOVE TO MY HUSBAND, Benjamin, for the endless support and encouragement. I felt so supported by you all the way through and I truly couldn't have done this without you. Thank you for celebrating me with such devotion and taking on all the extra life stuff during the writing process. Our relationship has taught me so much about love.

To Eva Avery, my editor, to whom I owe a world of thanks. Your gifts are also woven throughout this book. Deep bows to you for the emotional support and mountains of energy, structure, and attention you poured into this project with me. This was a powerful initiation for us both. In appreciation to the Chronicle team, Cecilia Santini, Tera Killip, Beth Weber, Pamela Geismar, and Michelle Triant, and to my agent, Johanna, at Writers House, for your efforts behind the scenes to bring this book to life.

To Andy, for bringing solar energy into Rising Woman and supporting us all. To Andrea, my dear friend and Rising Woman COO, and to the rest of my loyal team, Alissa, Tatiana, Georgianna, and Juno, you kept the business afloat and made it possible for me to do this. Chel, your love of details was my saving grace, and it was so much fun to work with you during this process. Thank you for all the early mornings and late nights spent on this project. To all of my readers and *Becoming the One* members who graciously gifted their stories to share in this book and who courageously embody these teachings in their own lives—I bow to you. Remembering my past social workers and foster parents—notably Janine, Lisa, and Alayne. It was you who held me through those dark times, and I will forever be grateful for your love and devotion to keeping me safe.

To my mom, who supported this book, thank you for giving me this life. Our journey together has propelled me to be in the most soul-fulfilling work, and I wouldn't change a thing.

Deep reverence to my past and present teachers, mentors, and guides: P. T. Mistlberger, Nikiah Seeds, Mark Wolynn, Harville Hendrix, Helen LaKelly Hunt, and Dr. Diane Poole Heller: My sincere appreciation for your work in the world and for all of the wisdom you share. An honorable mention must go to Nessi Gomes and Danit—your music was my soundtrack as I wrote this book. Thank you for singing me into communion with Spirit and connecting me to Source through your art. To all my extended friends and family who consistently checked in and sent me words of encouragement as I disappeared for a year, your love was received. In devotion to my ancestors, and my guides: Thank you for carrying me through and whispering your teachings in my ear.

RECOMMENDED READING

Adult Children of Emotionally Immature Parents by Lindsay C. Gibson, PhD

The Body Keeps the Score by Bessel Van Der Kolk, MD

Braiding Sweetgrass by Robin Wall Kimmerer

The Dance of Anger by Harriet Lerner, PhD

Getting the Love You Want by Harville Hendrix, PhD, and Helen LaKelly Hunt, PhD

Hold On to Your Kids by Gabor Maté and Gordon Neufeld

It Didn't Start with You by Mark Wolynn

The Journey from Abandonment to Healing by Susan Anderson

The Power of Attachment by Diane Poole Heller, PhD

The Sexual Healing Journey by Wendy Maltz

Women Who Run with the Wolves by Clarissa Pinkola Estés, PhD